70 YEARS OF POPULAR MUSIC
THE THIRTIES
PART THREE

Music processed by
Barnes Music Engraving Ltd, East Sussex TN22 4HA, UK

First published 1994
Updated edition 1996

AND THE ANGELS SING

Words by JOHNNY MERCER
Music by ZIGGIE ELMAN

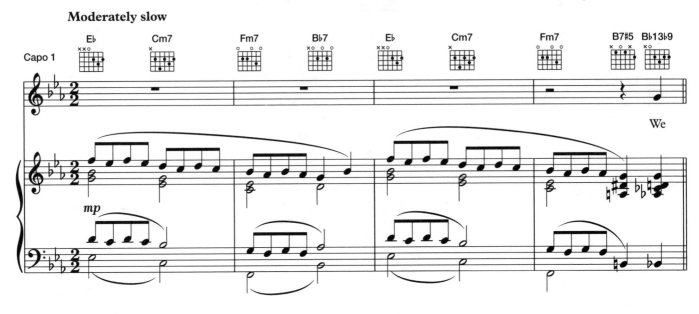

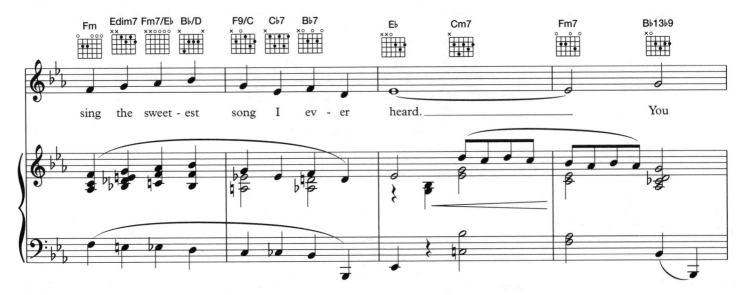

APRIL IN PARIS

Words by E Y HARBURG
Music by VERNON DUKE

Lyrics:

A-pril's in the air, but here in Pa - ris, A - pril wears a dif - ferent gown.

You can see her waltz - ing down the street, the tang of

8

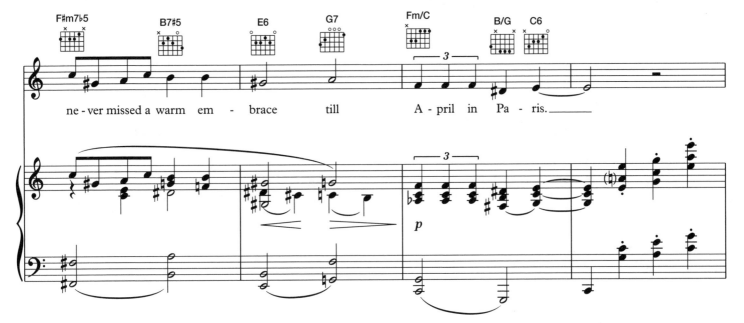

ne - ver missed a warm em - brace till A - pril in Pa - ris._____

Whom can I run to?_____ What have you done to_____ my

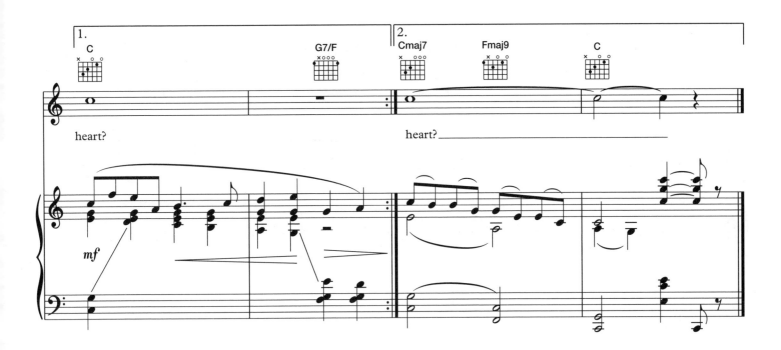

heart?   heart?_____

AUTUMN IN NEW YORK

Words and Music by VERNON DUKE

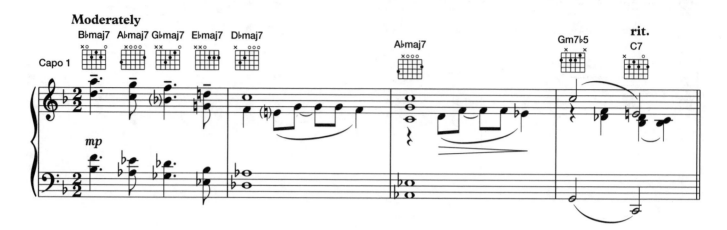

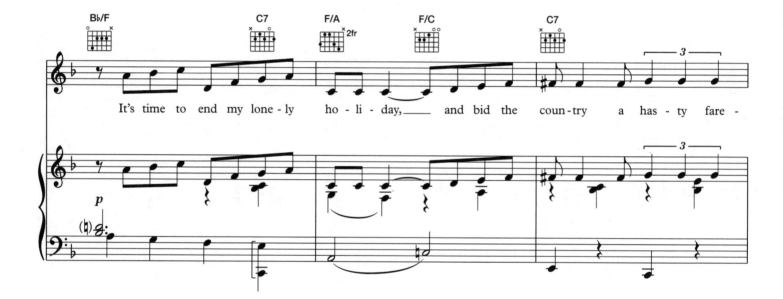

It's time to end my lone-ly ho-li-day,____ and bid the coun-try a has-ty fare-

-well. So on this grey and mel-an-cho-ly day, I'll

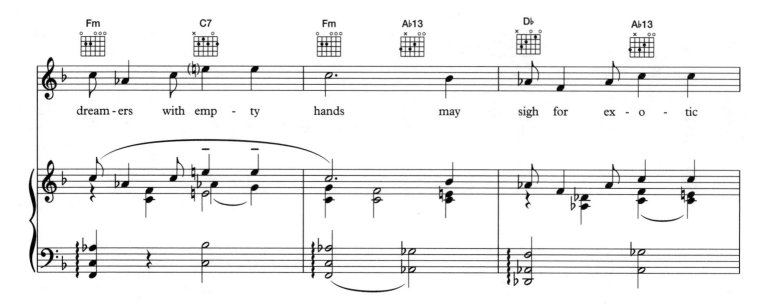

dream - ers   with emp - ty   hands   may   sigh   for   ex - o - tic

lands.   Au - tumn in New York,_____ it's good to live it a -

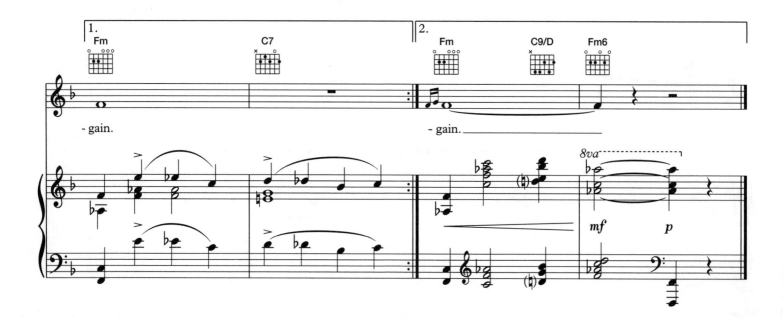

- gain.   - gain._____

BEGIN THE BEGUINE

Words and Music by COLE PORTER

ne - ver ne - ver to part._____ What

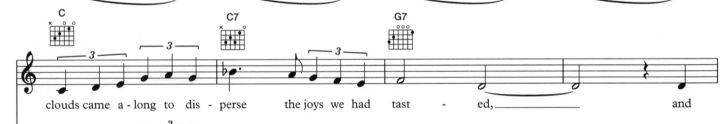

mo-ments di - vine,_____ what rap-tures se - rene,_____ till

clouds came a-long to dis - perse the joys we had tast - ed,_____ and

now when I hear peo-ple curse the chance that was wast - ed,_____ I

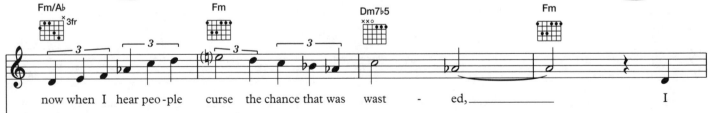

DANCING ON THE CEILING
(HE DANCES ON MY CEILING)

Words by LORENZ HART
Music by RICHARD RODGERS

LAZY BONES

Words and Music by JOHNNY MERCER and HOAGY CARMICHAEL
Additional Words by HORATIO NICHOLLS

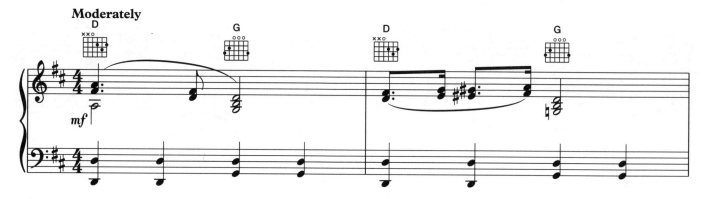

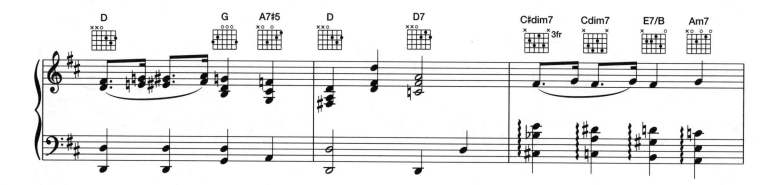

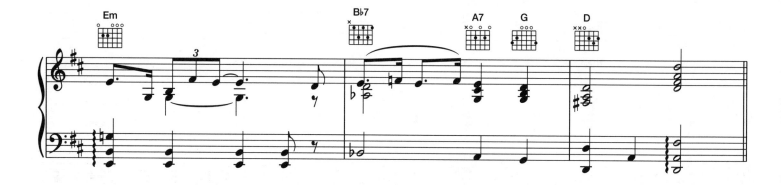

Long as there is chick-en gra-vy on your rice,___ ev-ery-thing is

Ne-ver in my life seen such a la-zy bones, sleep-ing all the

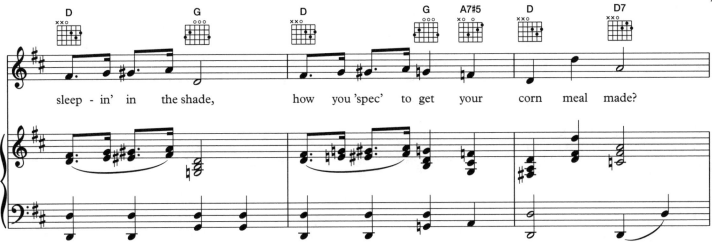

sleep - in' in the shade, how you 'spec' to get your corn meal made?

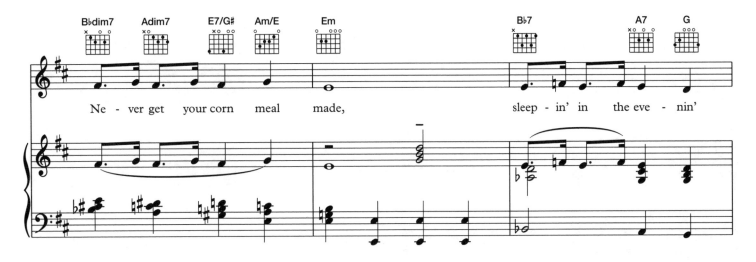

Ne - ver get your corn meal made, sleep - in' in the eve - nin'

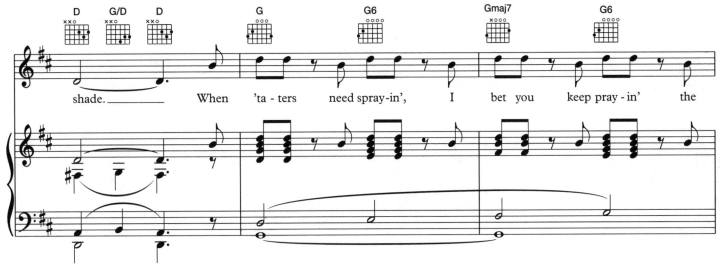

shade. _____ When 'ta - ters need spray-in', I bet you keep pray - in' the

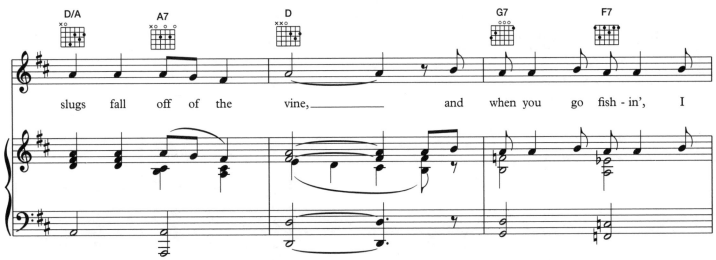

slugs fall off of the vine, _____ and when you go fish - in', I

EASY TO LOVE

Words and Music by COLE PORTER

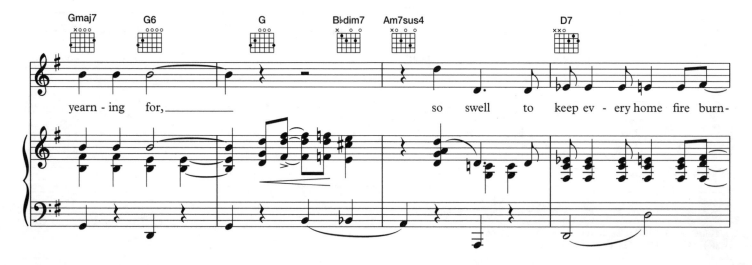

-ing for._____ We'd be so grand at the

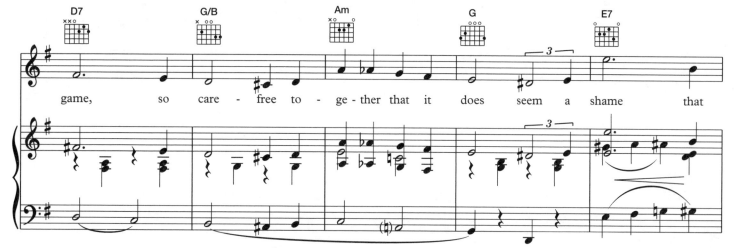

game, so care-free to-ge-ther that it does seem a shame that

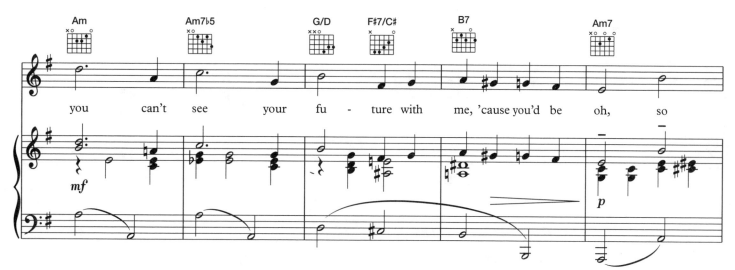

you can't see your fu-ture with me, 'cause you'd be oh, so

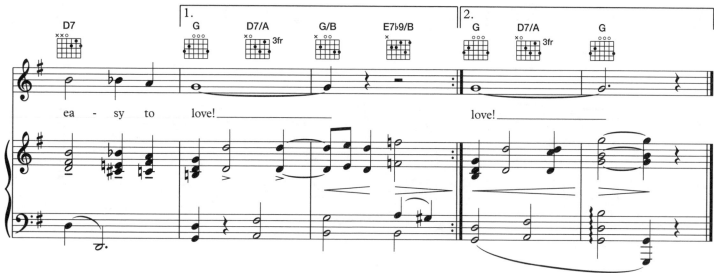

ea-sy to love!_____ love!_____

EXACTLY LIKE YOU

Words by DOROTHY FIELDS
Music by JIMMY McHUGH

Moderately

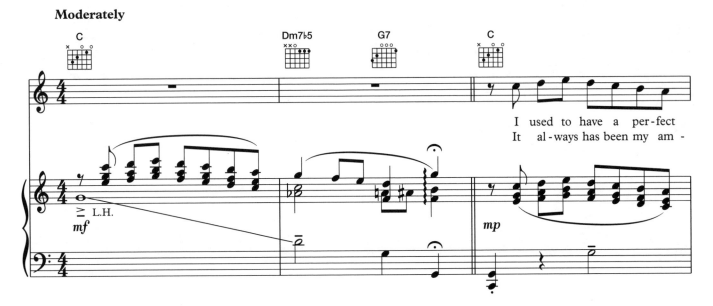

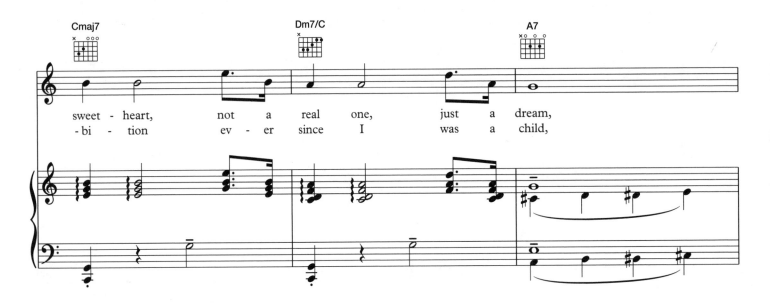

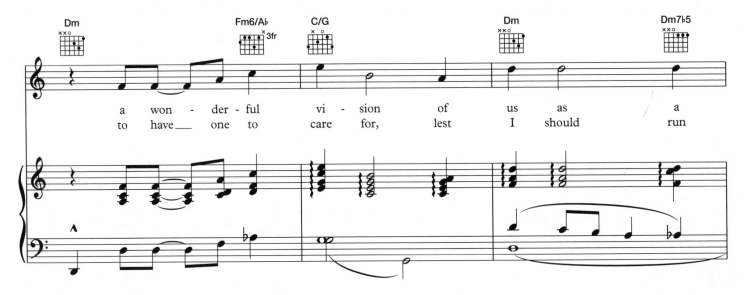

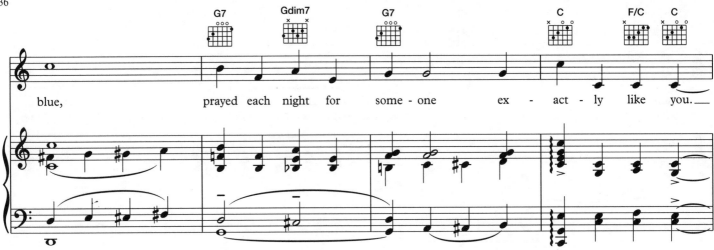

blue, prayed each night for some-one ex-act-ly like you.

Why should we spend mon-ey on a show or

two? No one does those love scenes ex-act-ly like you.

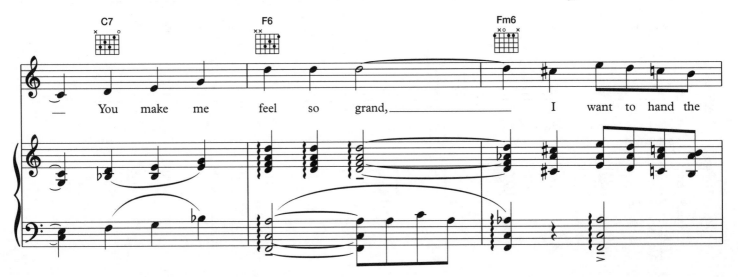

You make me feel so grand, I want to hand the

world to you._____ You seem to un-der-stand_____ each fool-ish lit-tle

scheme I'm schem - ing, dream I'm dream - ing. Now I know why

mo - ther taught me to be true, she meant me for

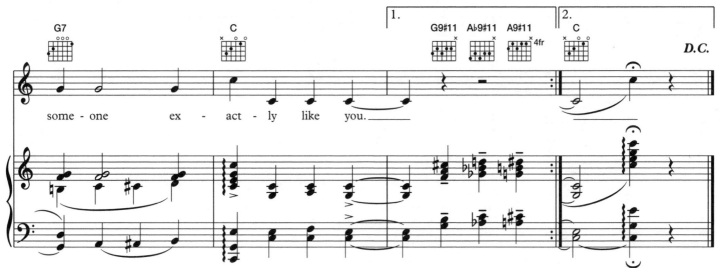

some - one ex - act - ly like you._____

A FINE ROMANCE

Words by DOROTHY FIELDS
Music by JEROME KERN

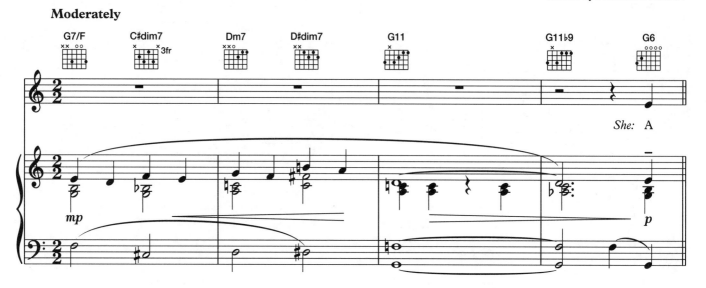

won't   wres - tle!   I   might   as   well   play   bridge with my   old   maid
all   mor - als!   I've ne - ver mussed   the   crease in your blue serge

aunts!   I   have - n't got   a   chance,   this   is   a   fine   ro -
pants,   I   ne - ver get   the   chance,   this   is   a   fine   ro -

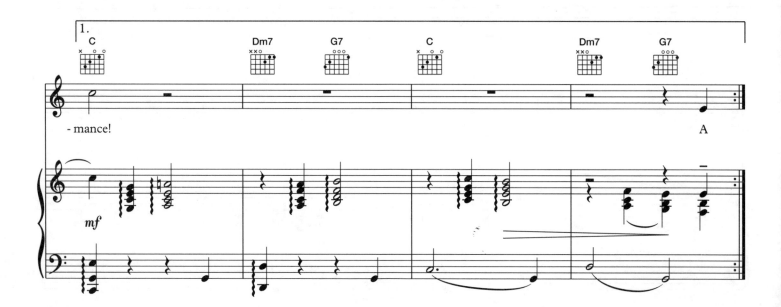

- mance!   A

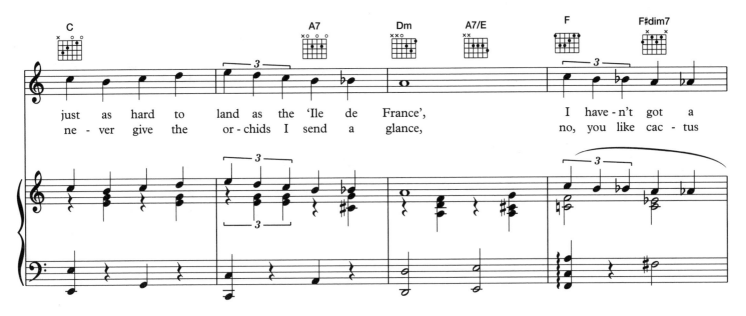

just as hard to land as the 'Ile de France',
ne - ver give the or - chids I send a glance,
I have - n't got a
no, you like cac - tus

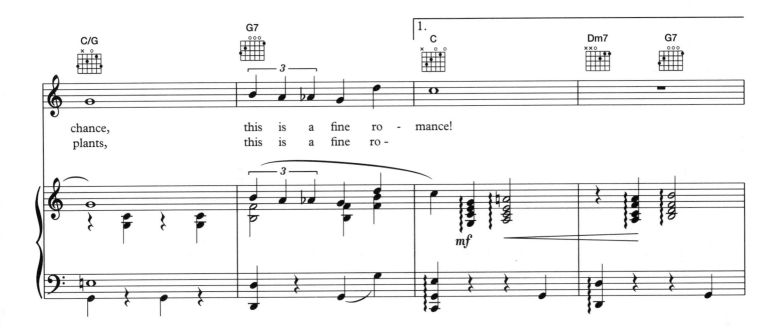

chance,
plants,
this is a fine ro - mance!
this is a fine ro -

1.

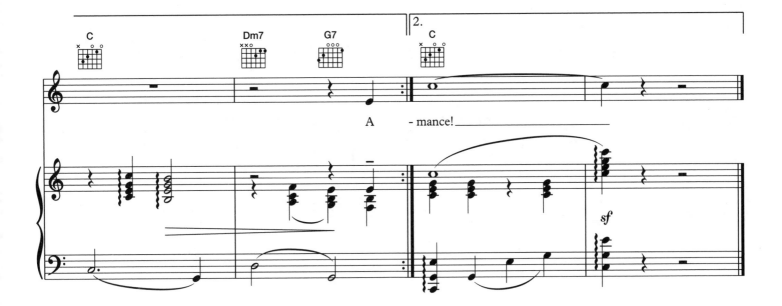

2.

A - mance! _____

GOOD MORNING

Words by ARTHUR FREED
Music by NACIO HERB BROWN

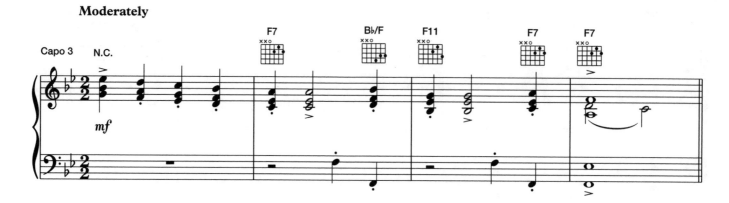

Here we are to-ge-ther, a cou-ple of stay-er up-pers, our

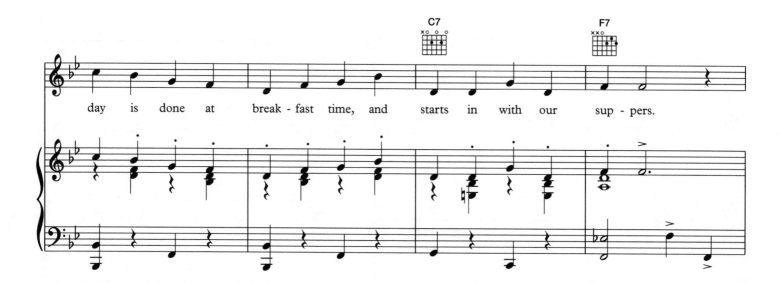

day is done at break-fast time, and starts in with our sup-pers.

Here we are to - ge - ther, but the best of friends must part, so

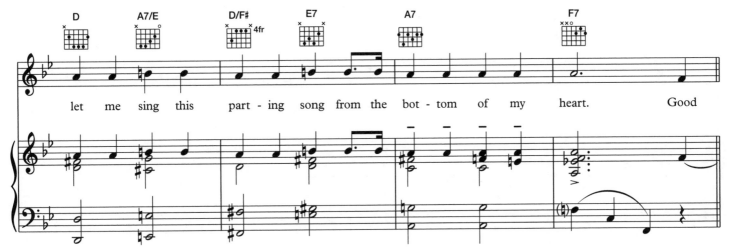

let me sing this part - ing song from the bot - tom of my heart. Good

morn - ing, good morn - ing, we've danced the

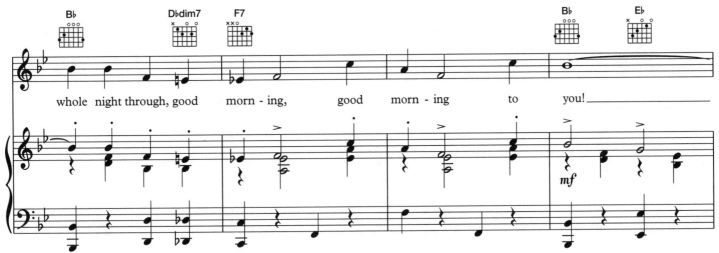

whole night through, good morn - ing, good morn - ing to you!_____

Good morn - ing, good morn - ing, it's great to

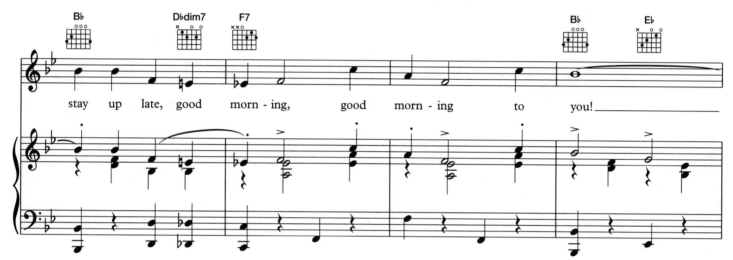

stay up late, good morn - ing, good morn - ing to you! _____

When the band be - gan to play, the

stars were shin - ing bright, now the milk - man's

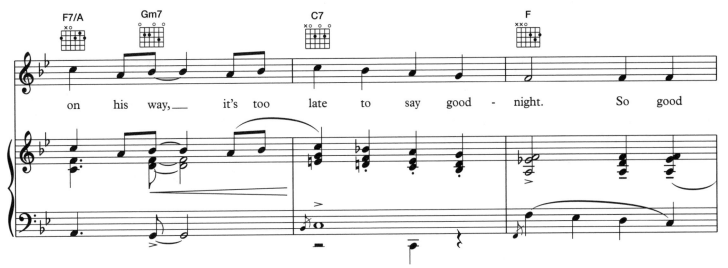

on his way,___ it's too late to say good - night. So good

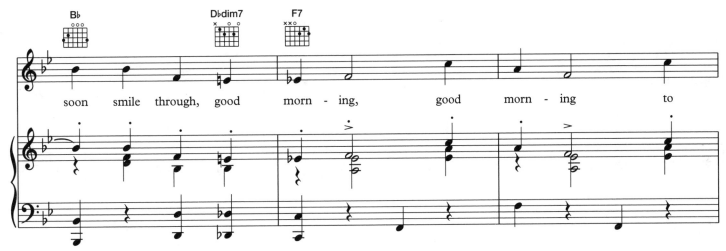

morn - ing, good morn - ing, sun - beams will

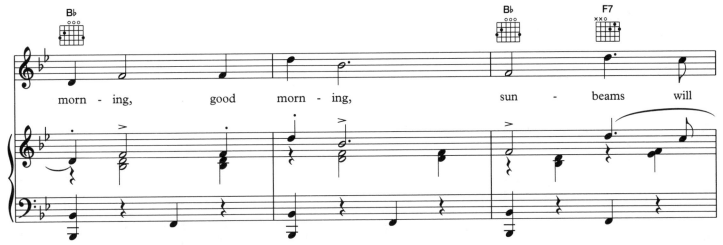

soon smile through, good morn - ing, good morn - ing to

1. you!___ 2. Good you!___

HARBOUR LIGHTS

Words and Music by JIMMY KENNEDY and HUGH WILLIAMS

eve-ning long a-go, a big ship was leav-ing, one eve-ning long a-go, two

lov-ers were griev-ing. A crim-son sun went down, the lights be-gan to glow

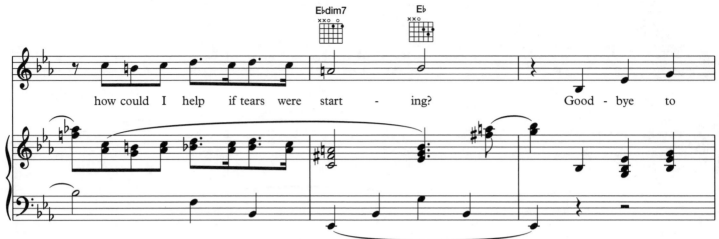

how could I help if tears were start - ing? Good - bye to

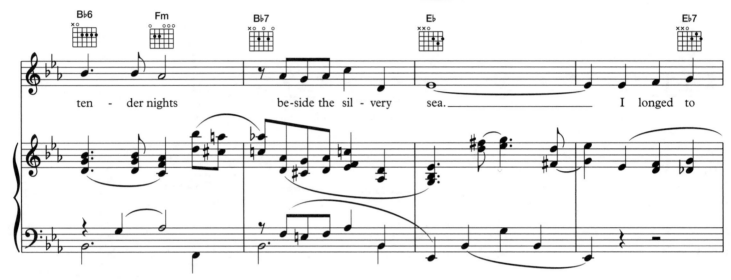

ten - der nights be-side the sil - very sea._____ I longed to

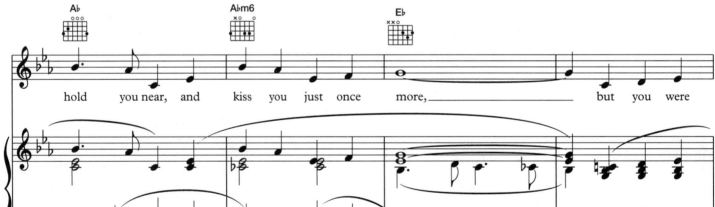

hold you near, and kiss you just once more,_____ but you were

on the ship, and I was on the shore._____ Now I know

lone - ly nights,   for all the while my heart is whis - pering

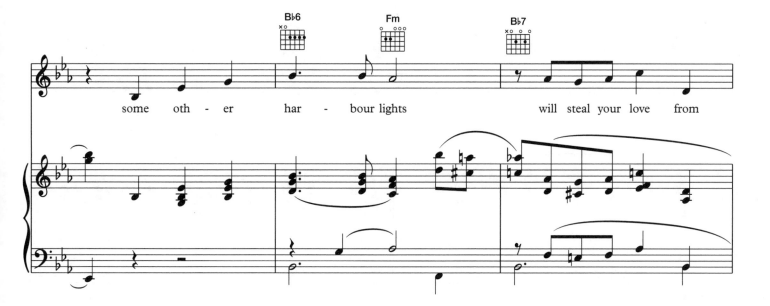

some oth - er har - bour lights   will steal your love from

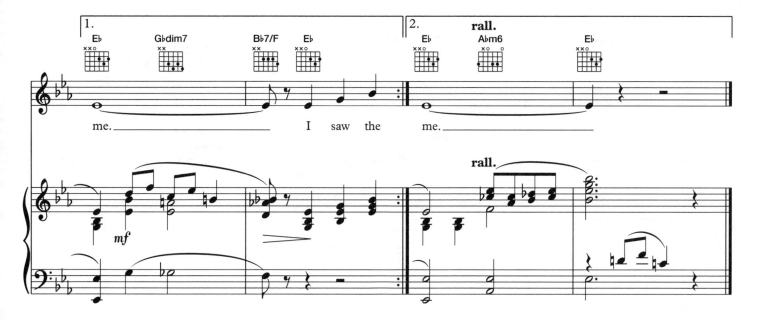

me. _____ I saw the   me. _____

HAVE YOU EVER BEEN LONELY

Words by GEORGE BROWN
Music by PETER DE ROSE

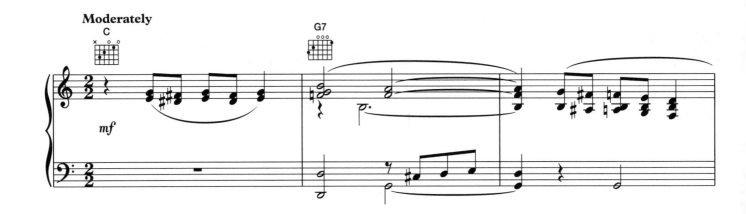

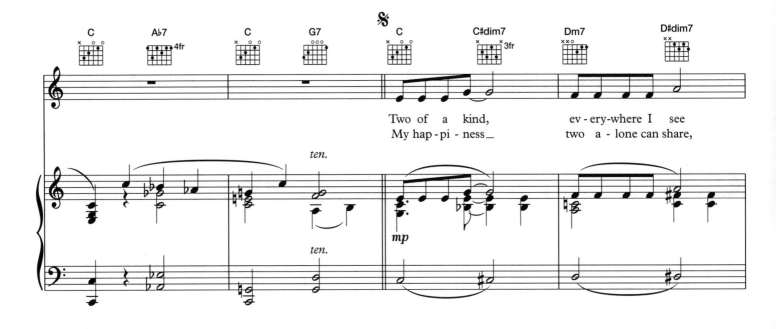

Two of a kind, ev-ery-where I see
My hap-pi-ness two a-lone can share,

lov-ers in the moon-light, rob-ins in a tree. Now that we have part-ed,
now that I have lost you life is hard to bear. You and I have quar-relled,

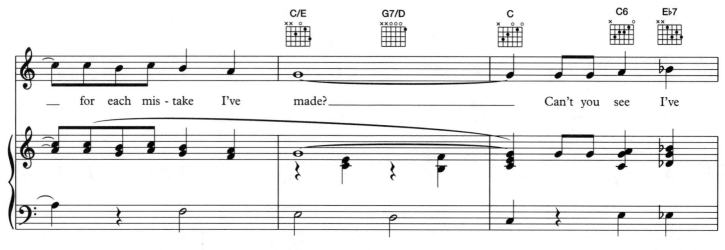

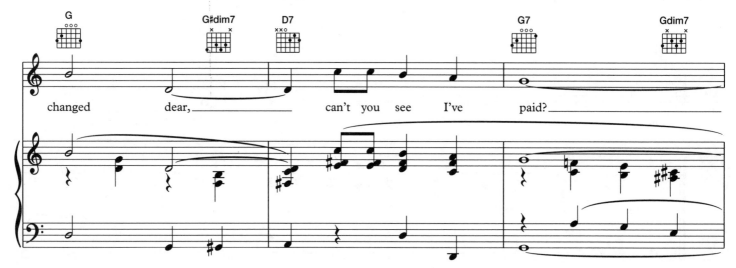

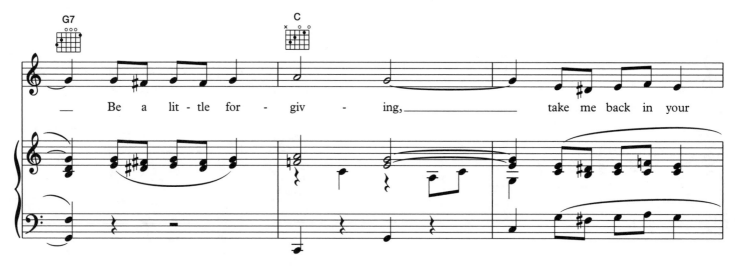

HEAR MY SONG, VIOLETTA

Original Words by OTHMAR KLOSE
English Words by HARRY S PEPPER
Music by OTHMAR KLOSE and RUDOLF LUCKESCH

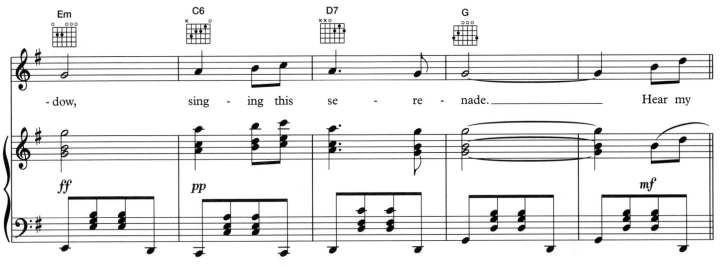

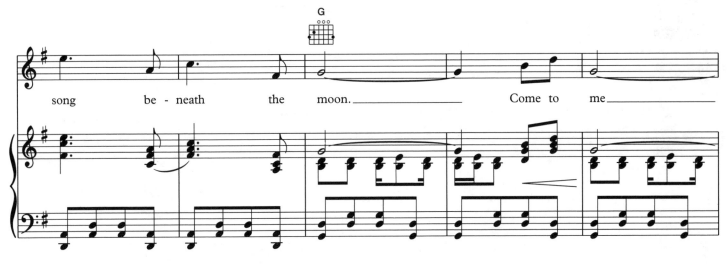

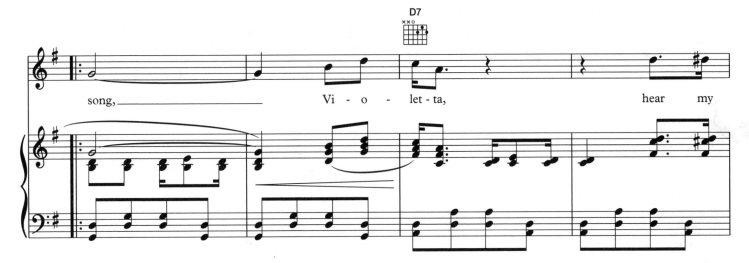

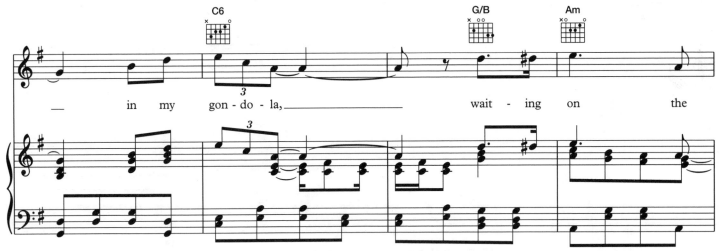

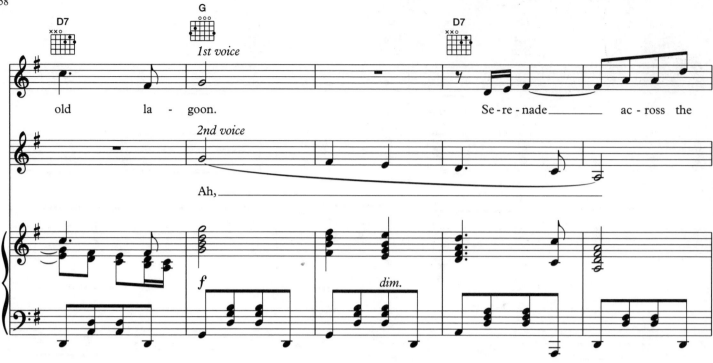

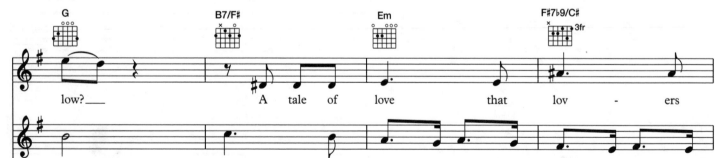

sang   long   a - go.   Hear my song_____

sing so long a - go.

_____ in my gon-do-la,_____   wait - ing on   the

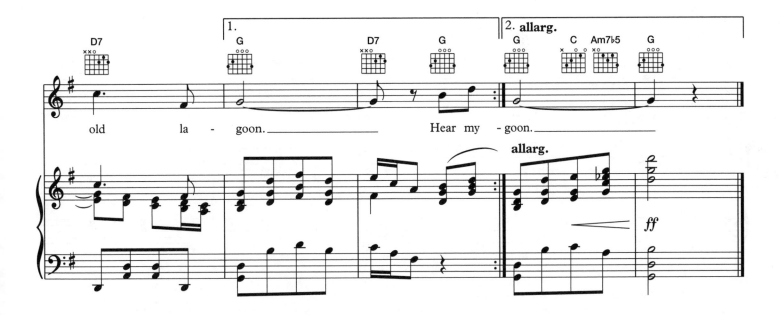

old   la - goon._____   Hear my - goon._____

IF

Words by ROBERT HARGREAVES and STANLEY DAMERELL
Music by TOLCHARD EVANS

You are my sweet i - deal,_____
I've made for you a shrine_____

and at your feet I kneel._____
in this poor heart of mine,_____

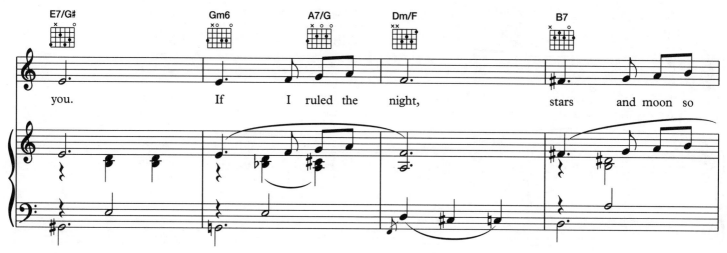

you. If I ruled the night, stars and moon so

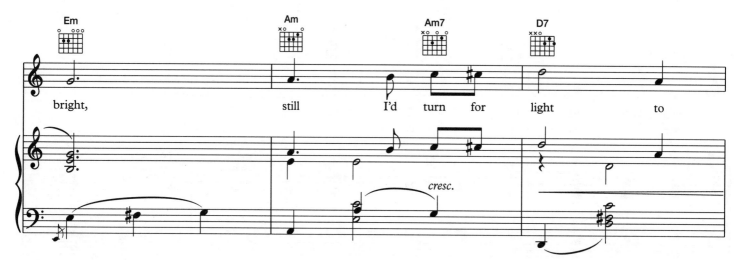

bright, still I'd turn for light to

you. _____ If the world to me bowed, yet hum-bly I'd

plead to you, if my friends were a crowd, I'd turn in my

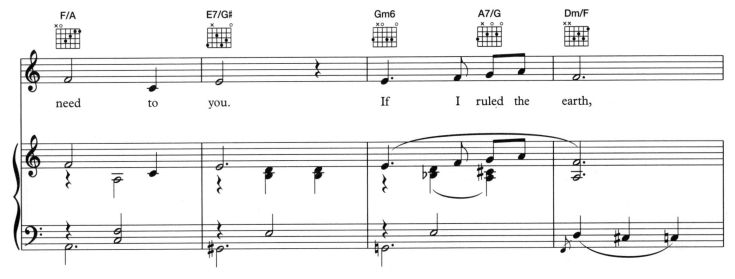

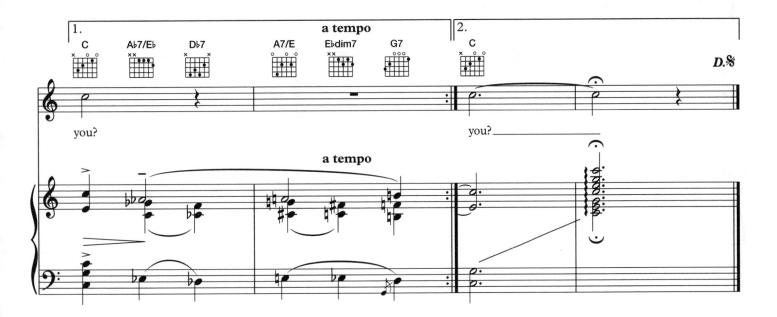

I GET A KICK OUT OF YOU

Words and Music by COLE PORTER

I get no kick___ from cham - pagne,_____ mere al-co-hol

— does-n't thrill me at all,___ so tell me why

— should it be true_____ that I get a kick

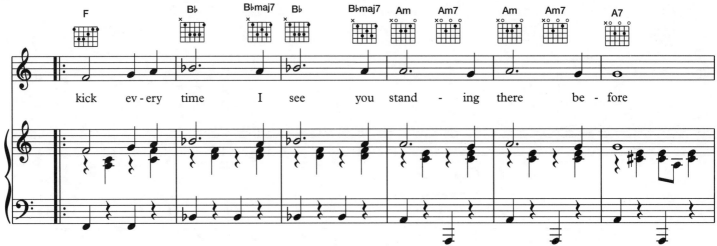

kick ev - ery time I see you stand - ing there be - fore

me, I get a kick___ though it's pa - tent - ly clear_____ that you

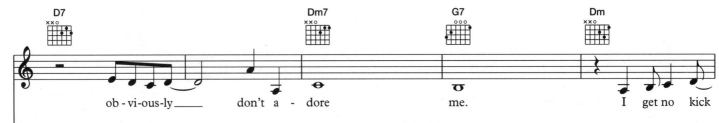

ob - vi - ous - ly___ don't a - dore me. I get no kick

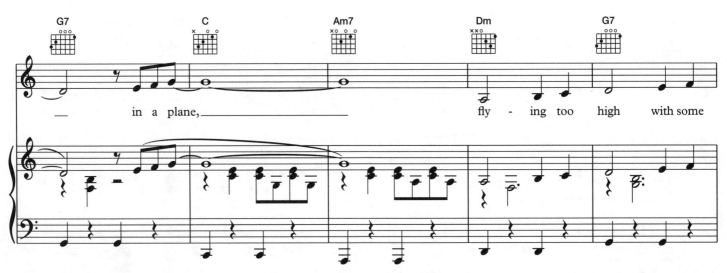

__ in a plane,_____ fly - ing too high with some

67

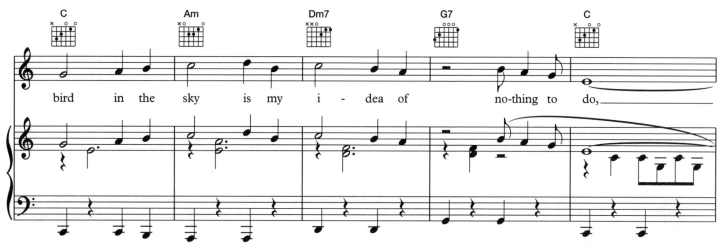

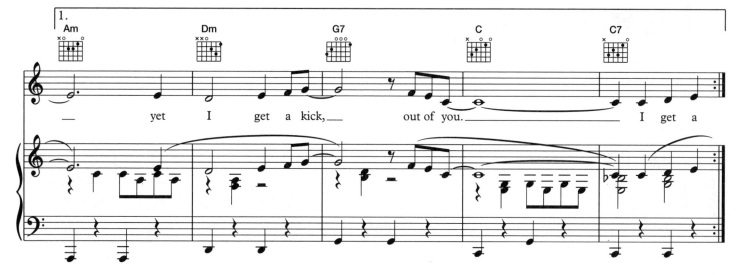

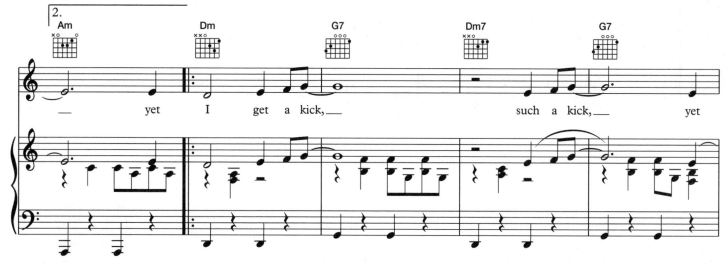

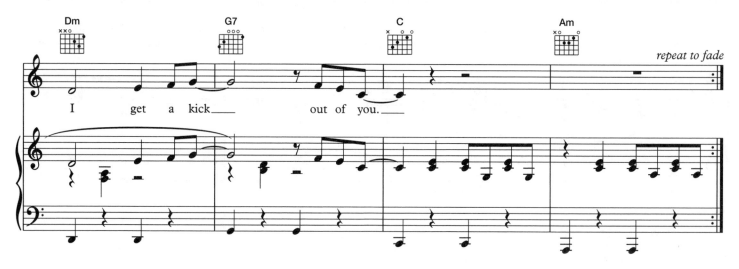

I SURRENDER DEAR

Words by GORDON CLIFFORD
Music by HARRY BARRIS

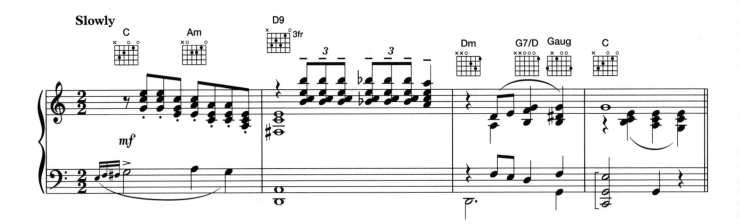

Pride, sad splen-did li - ar, sworn e - ne-my of
I can't live with-out you, though once I bade you

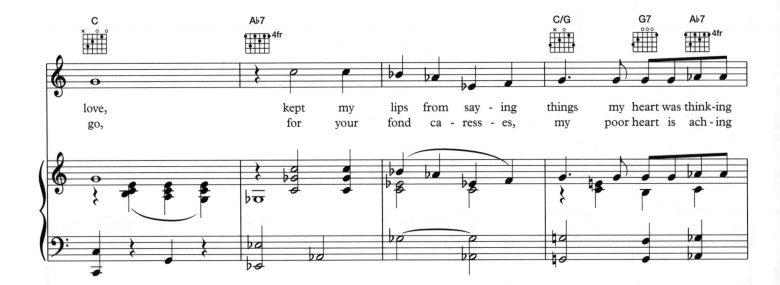

love, kept my lips from say-ing things my heart was think-ing
go, for your fond ca - ress - es, my poor heart is ach-ing

I may seem proud, I may act gay, it's just a pose,

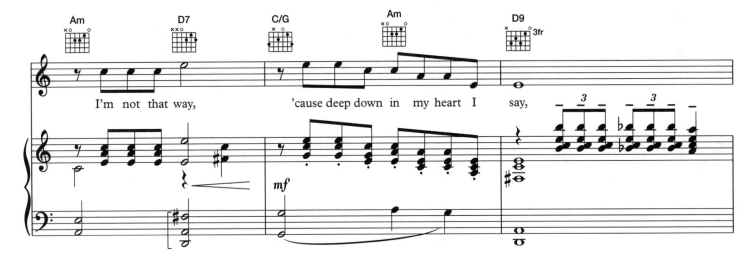

I'm not that way, 'cause deep down in my heart I say,

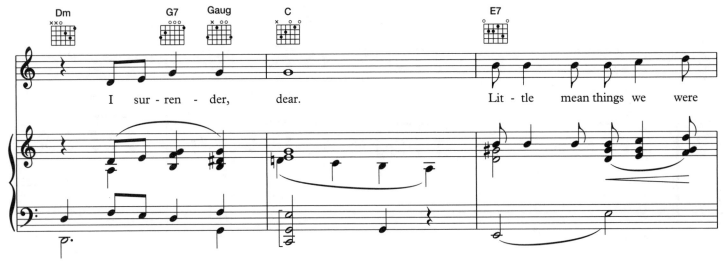

I sur - ren - der, dear. Lit - tle mean things we were

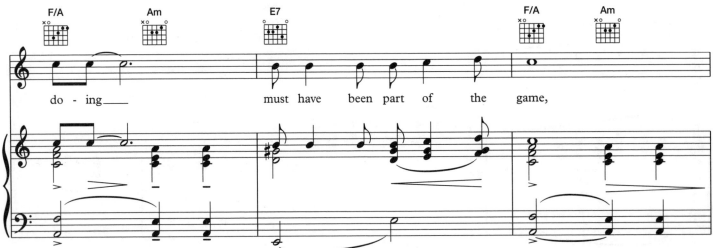

do - ing____ must have been part of the game,

IT'S DE-LOVELY

Words and Music by COLE PORTER

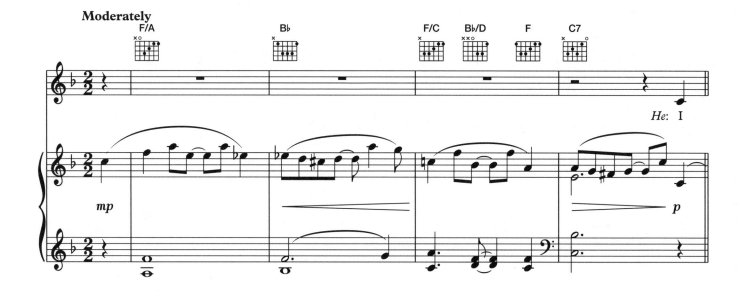

He: I feel a sud-den urge to sing___ the kind of dit-ty that in-vokes the spring, so con-

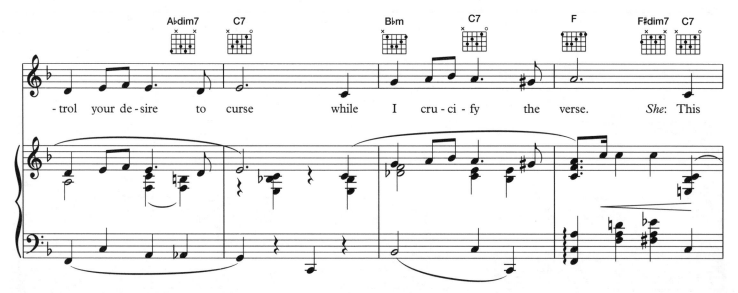

-trol your de-sire to curse while I cru-ci-fy the verse. She: This

verse I've start - ed seems to me__ the Tin Pan ti - the - sis of me - lo - dy,__ so to

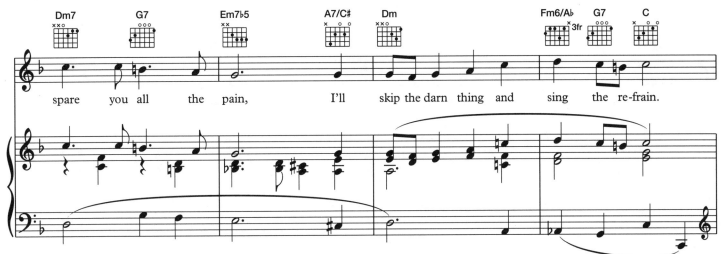

spare you all the pain, I'll skip the darn thing and sing the re-frain.

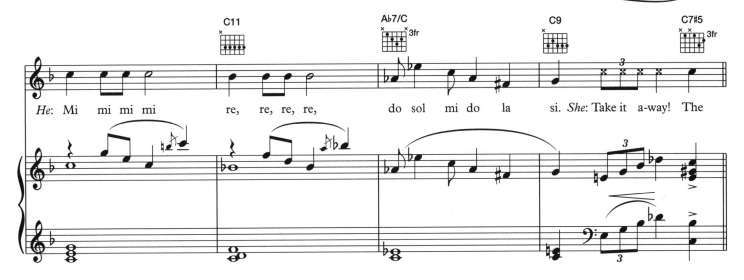

He: Mi mi mi mi re, re, re, re, do sol mi do la si. *She:* Take it a-way! The

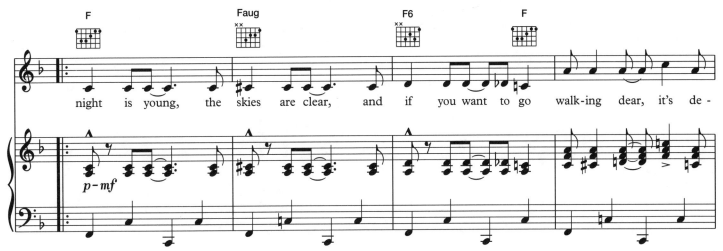

night is young, the skies are clear, and if you want to go walk-ing dear, it's de-

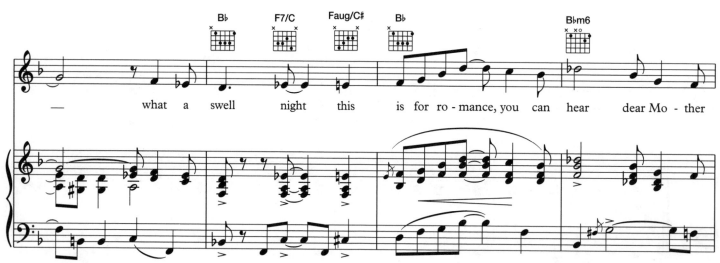

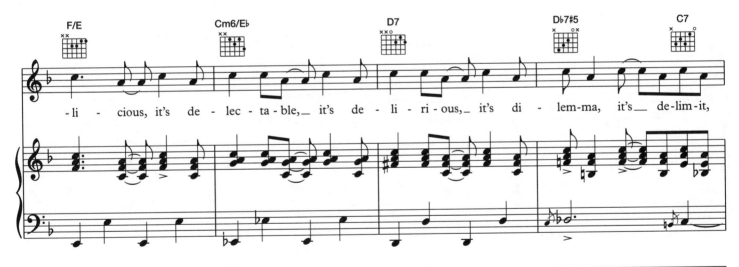

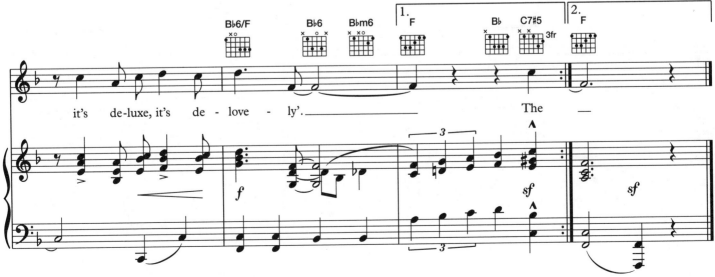

IT'S EASY TO REMEMBER

Words by LORENZ HART
Music by RICHARD RODGERS

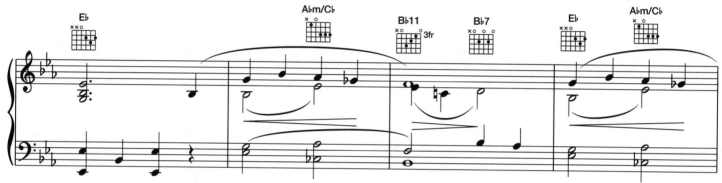

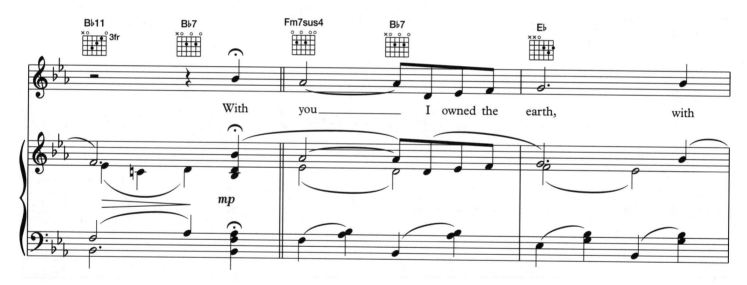

With you _____ I owned the earth, with

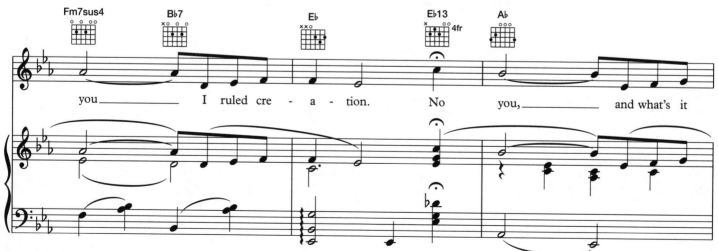

you _____ I ruled cre - a - tion. No you, _____ and what's it

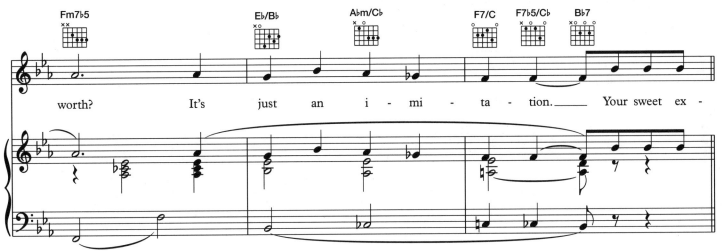

worth? It's just an i - mi - ta - tion._____ Your sweet ex -

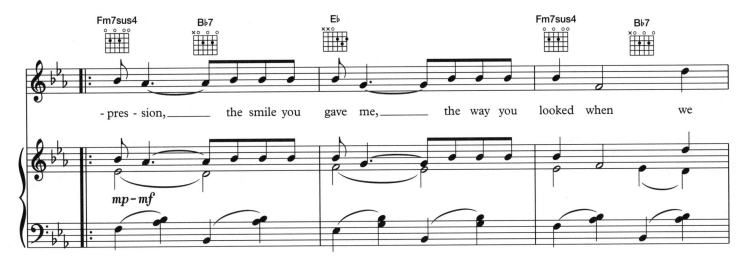

- pres - sion,_____ the smile you gave me,_____ the way you looked when we

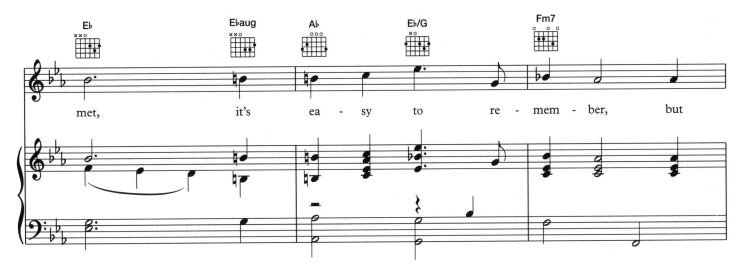

met, it's ea - sy to re - mem - ber, but

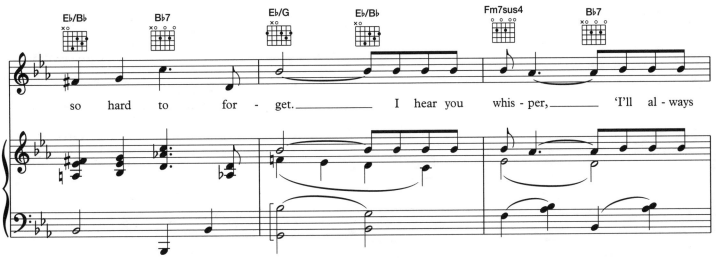

so hard to for - get._____ I hear you whis - per,_____ 'I'll al - ways

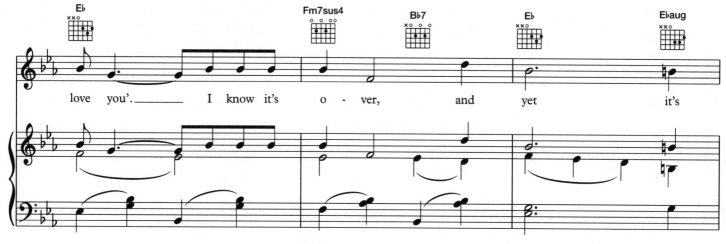

love you'._____ I know it's o - ver, and yet it's

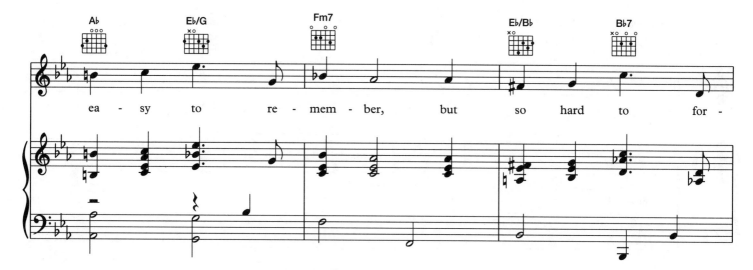

ea - sy to re - mem - ber, but so hard to for -

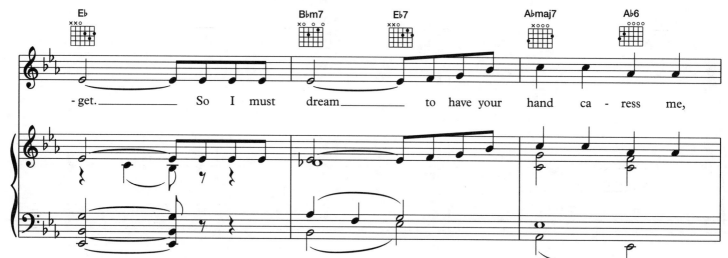

- get._____ So I must dream_____ to have your hand ca - ress me,

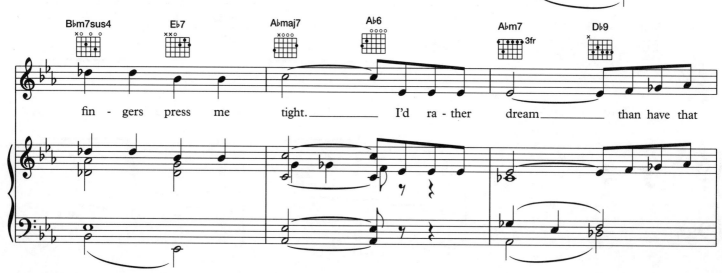

fin - gers press me tight._____ I'd ra - ther dream_____ than have that

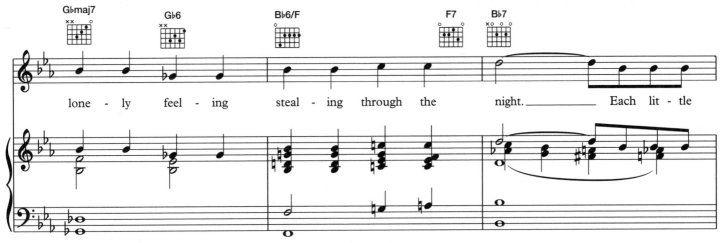

lone - ly feel - ing steal - ing through the night._____ Each lit - tle

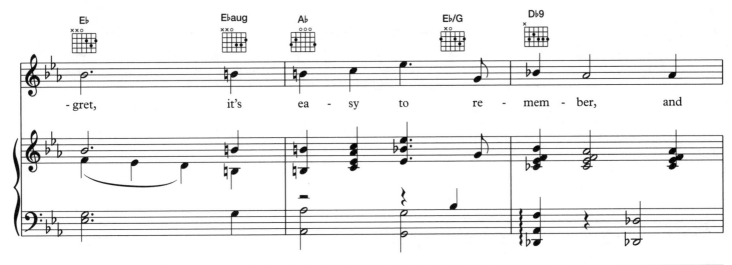

mo - ment_____ is clear be - fore me,_____ and though it brings me re -

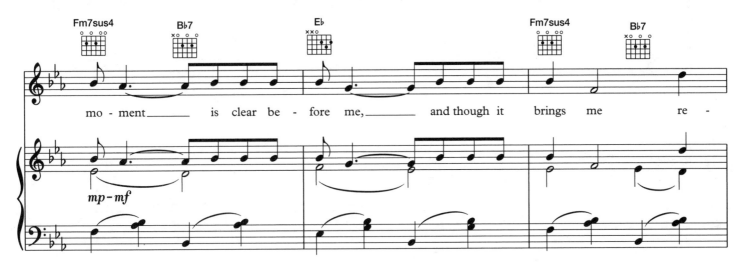

- gret, it's ea - sy to re - mem - ber, and

so hard to for - get._____ Your sweet ex - so hard to for - get.

LADY OF SPAIN

Words by STANLEY DAMERELL and ROBERT HARGREAVES
Music by TOLCHARD EVANS

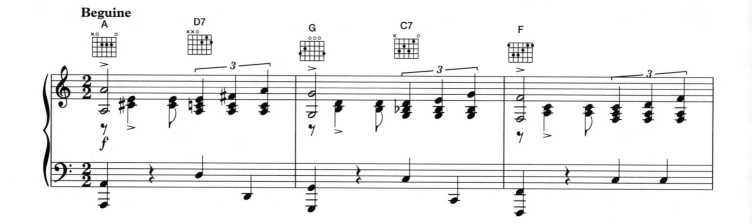

Night in Ma - drid, blue and ten - der,_____

— Span - ish moon makes sil - ver splen-dour,_____

mu - sic throb-bing, plain - tive sob-bing

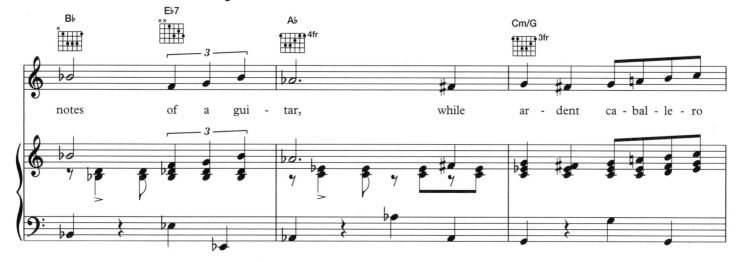

notes   of a gui-tar,   while ar-dent ca-bal-le-ro

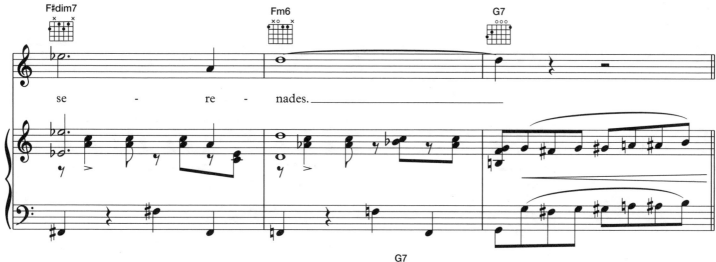

se - re - nades._____

La - dy of Spain, I a-dore you,_____

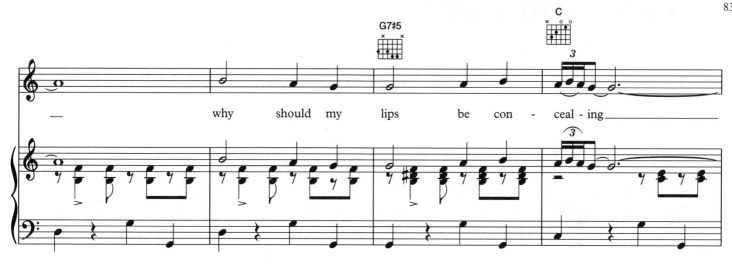

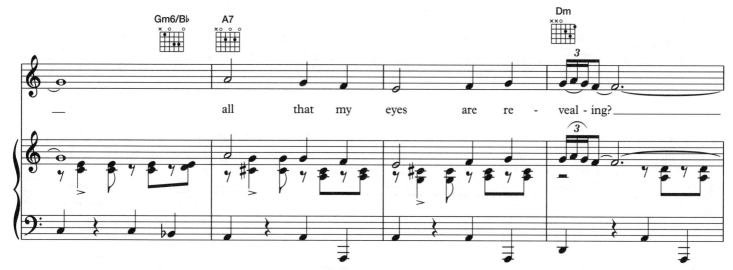

LITTLE WHITE LIES

Words and Music by WALTER DONALDSON

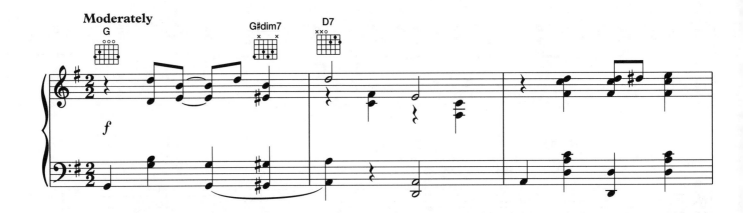

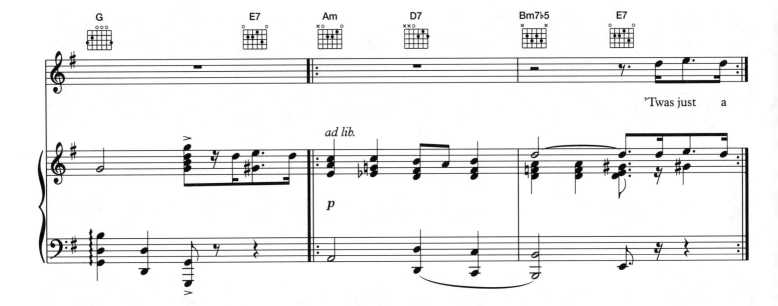

'Twas just a

night like this, filled with bliss, __ you led my heart a - stray, __

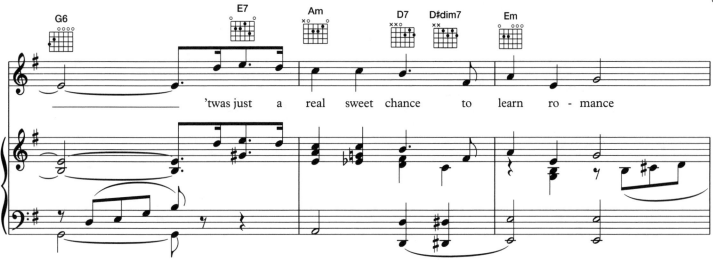

'twas just a real sweet chance to learn ro-mance

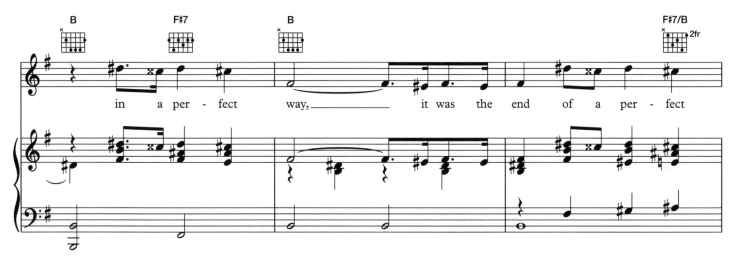

in a per-fect way,_____ it was the end of a per-fect

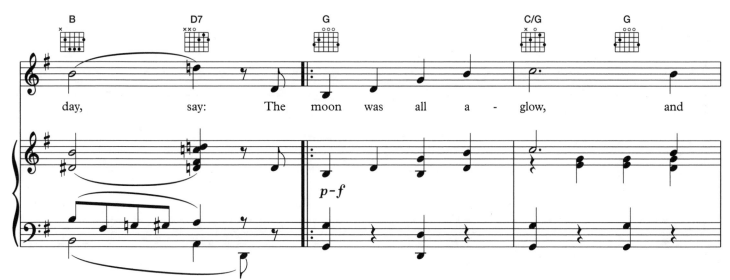

day, say: The moon was all a-glow, and

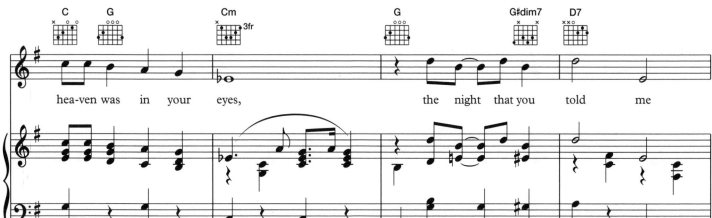

hea-ven was in your eyes, the night that you told me

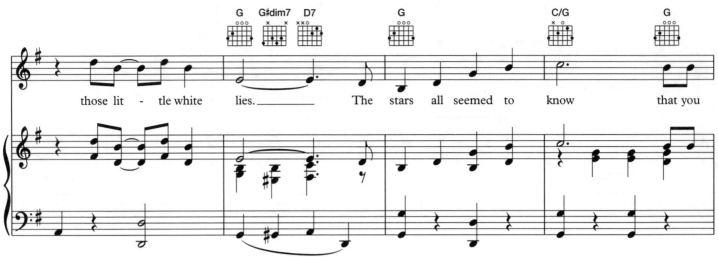

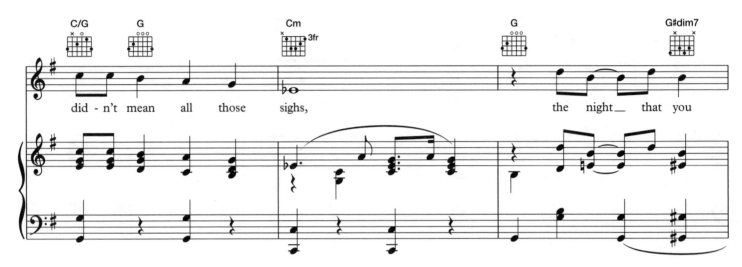

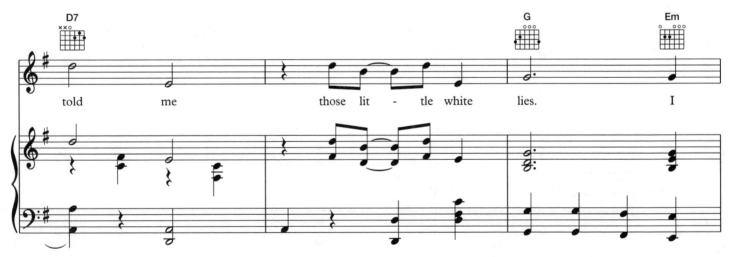

LOVE WALKED IN

Music and Lyrics by GEORGE GERSHWIN and IRA GERSHWIN

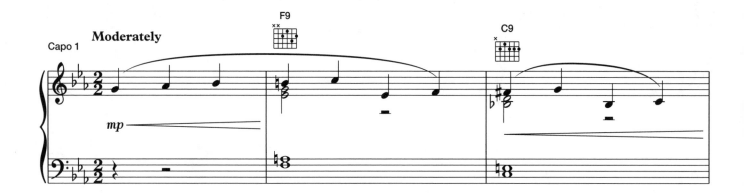

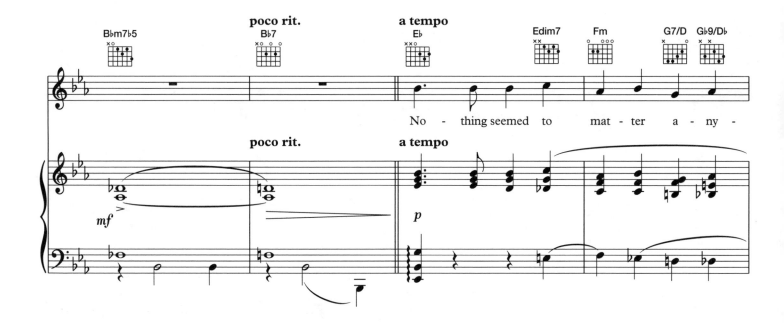

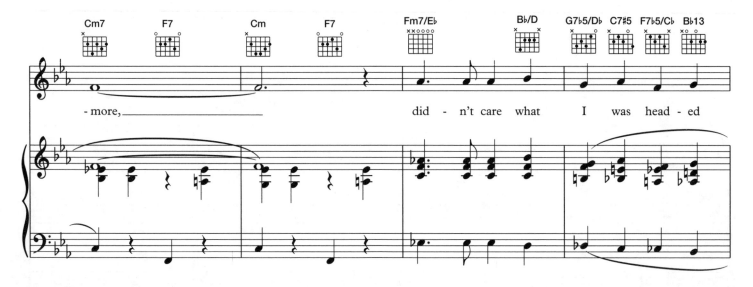

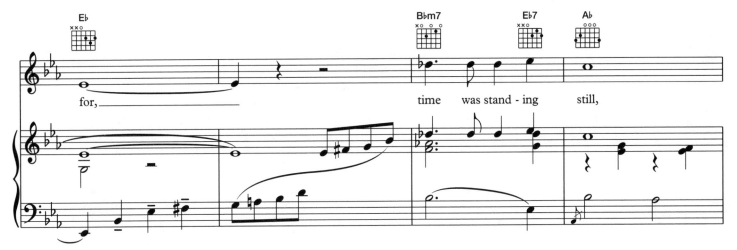

for,_____ time was stand-ing still,

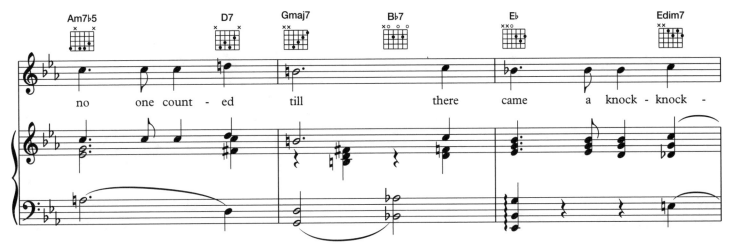

no one count-ed till there came a knock-knock-

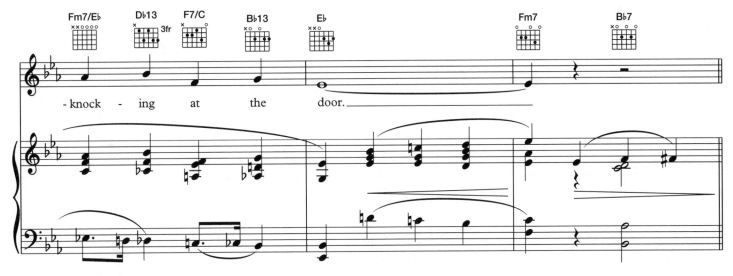

-knock-ing at the door._____

slowly

Love walked right in and drove the sha-dows a-way,

LOVE'S LAST WORD IS SPOKEN

English Words by BRUCE SIEVIER
Italian Words by ENNIO NERI
Music by C A BIXIO

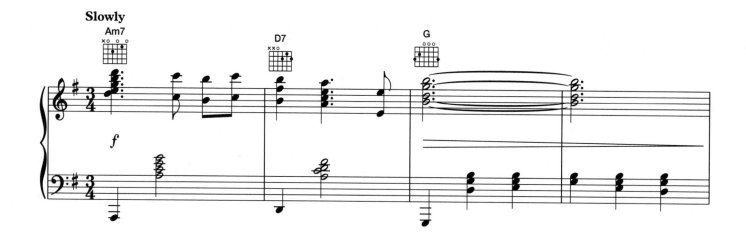

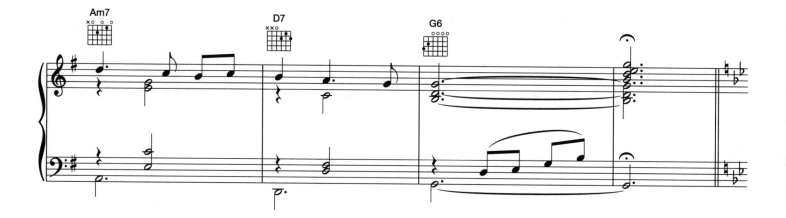

Do you re-mem-ber a night in Sep-tem-ber, my
Our hearts were ma-ted, but now we are fa-ted to
Co - me sei bel - la, più bel - la sta - se - ra Ma -
So che u - na bel-lae ma - liar - da si - re - na sei

own?
part.
- *riù:*
tu;

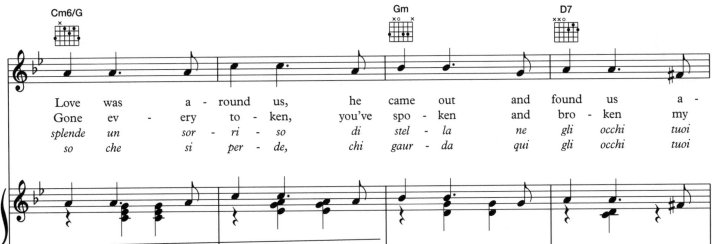

Love was a - round us, he came out and found us a -
Gone ev - ery to - ken, you've spo - ken and bro - ken my
splende un sor - ri - so di stel - la ne gli occhi tuoi
so che si per - de, chi gaur - da qui gli occhi tuoi

- lone.
heart.
blù!
blù!

Now he has left us, be - reft us of all we es -
I'm face to face with dis - grace and with lone - li - ness
An - che se av - ver - soil de - sti - no do - ma - ni sa -
Ma che m'im - por - ta se il mon - do si bur - la di

- teemed.
too.
- rà,
me?

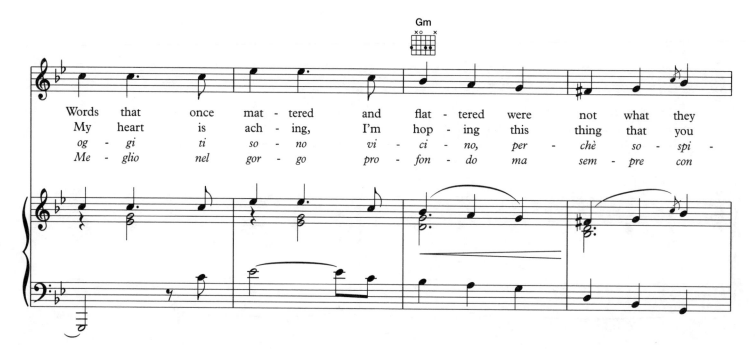

Words that once mat - tered and flat - tered were not what they
My heart is ach - ing, I'm hop - ing this thing that you
og - gi ti so - no vi - ci - no, per - chè so - spi -
Me - glio nel gor - go pro - fon - do ma sem - pre con

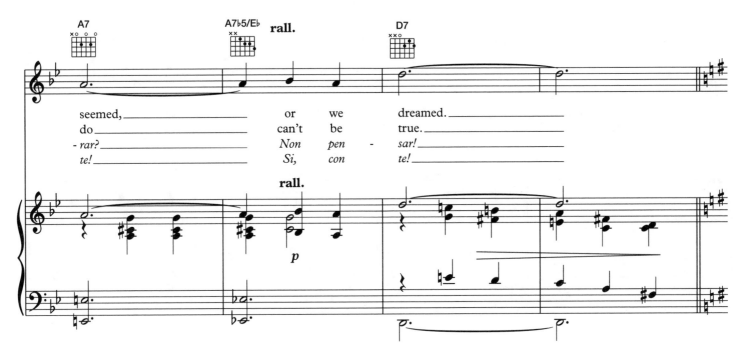

seemed,＿＿＿＿＿＿ or we dreamed.＿＿＿＿＿
do＿＿＿＿＿＿ can't be true.＿＿＿＿＿
- rar?＿＿＿＿＿ Non pen - sar!＿＿＿＿＿
te!＿＿＿＿＿＿ Si, con te!＿＿＿＿＿

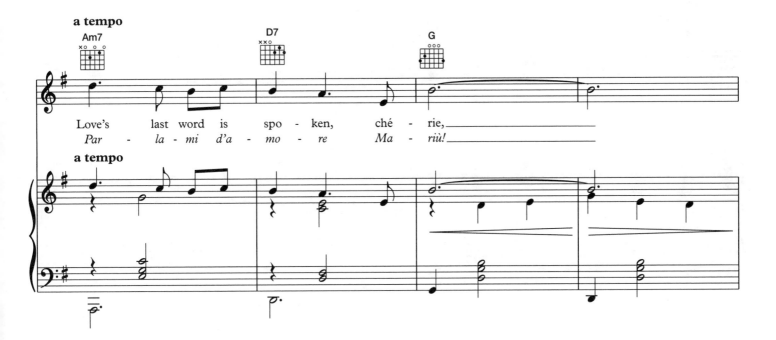

Love's last word is spo - ken, ché - rie,＿＿＿＿＿
Par - la - mi d'a - mo - re Ma - riù!＿＿＿＿＿

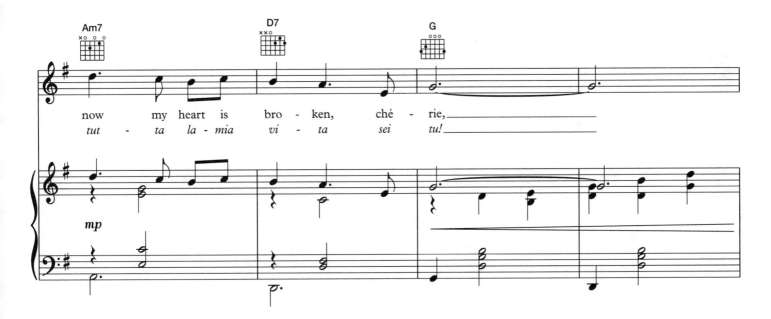

now my heart is bro - ken, ché - rie,＿＿＿＿＿
tut - ta la - mia vi - ta sei tu!＿＿＿＿＿

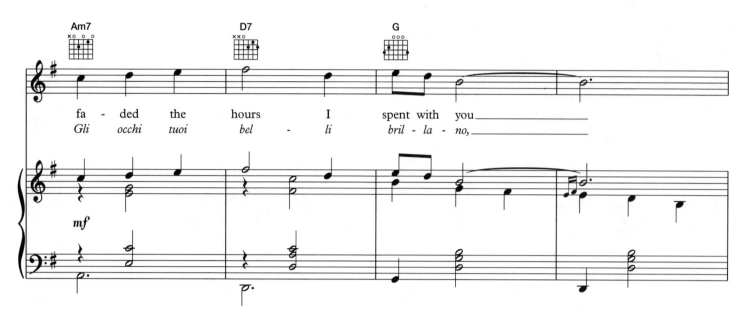

fa - ded the hours I spent with you_____
Gli occhi tuoi bel - li bril - la - no,_____

roam - ing the boule - vards, con - tent with you._____
fiamme di so - gno scin - til - la - no!_____

Once our hearts were blend - ed, ché - rie,_____
Dim - me che illu - sio - ne non è;_____

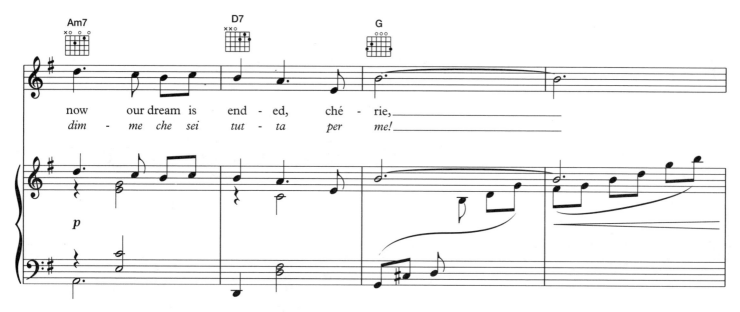

now our dream is end - ed, ché - rie,_____
*dim - me che sei tut - ta per me!*_____

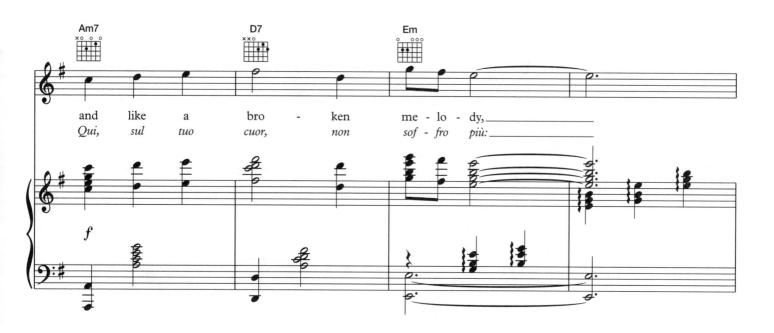

and like a bro - ken me - lo - dy,_____
*Qui, sul tuo cuor, non sof - fro più:*_____

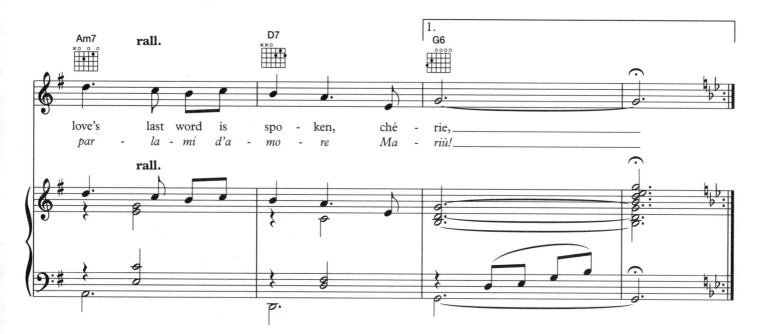

love's last word is spo - ken, ché - rie,_____
*par - la - mi d'a - mo - re Ma - riù!*_____

NIGHT AND DAY

Words and Music by COLE PORTER

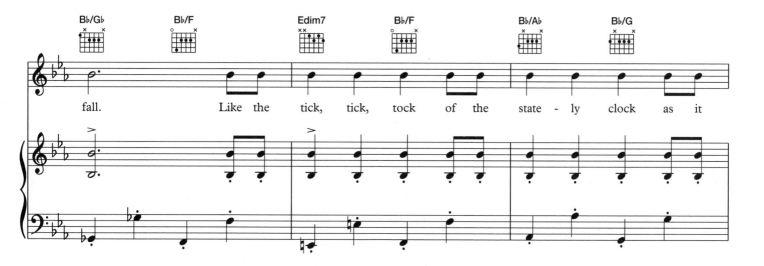

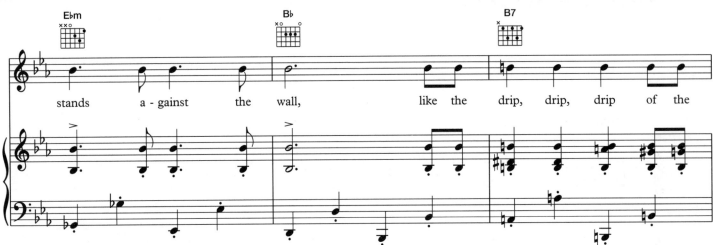

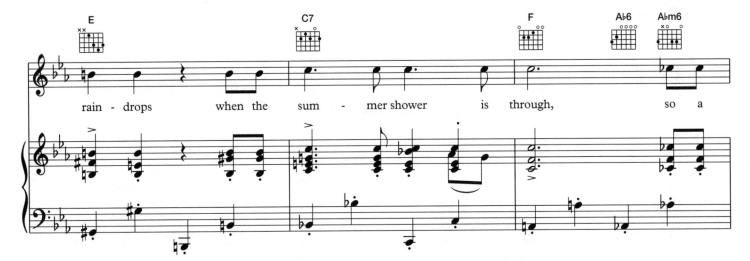

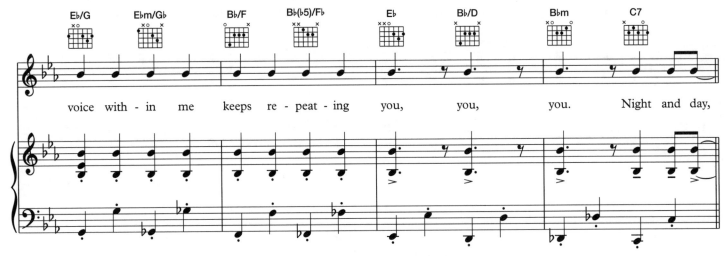

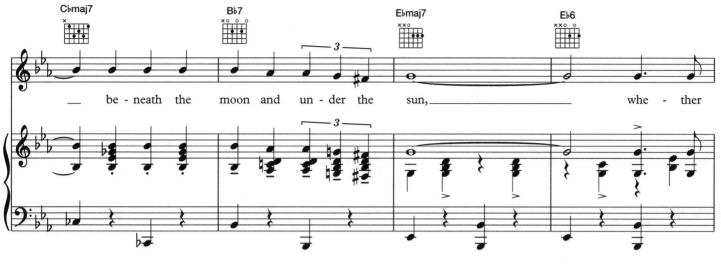

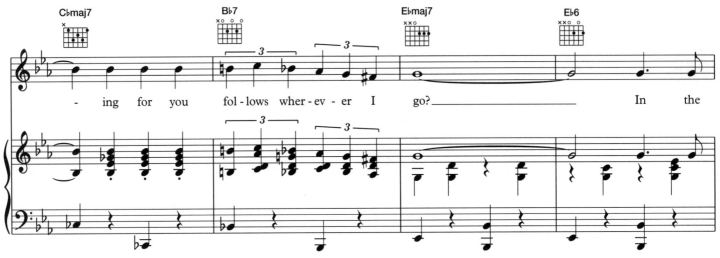

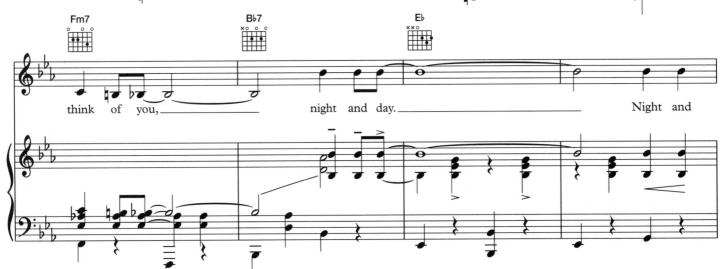

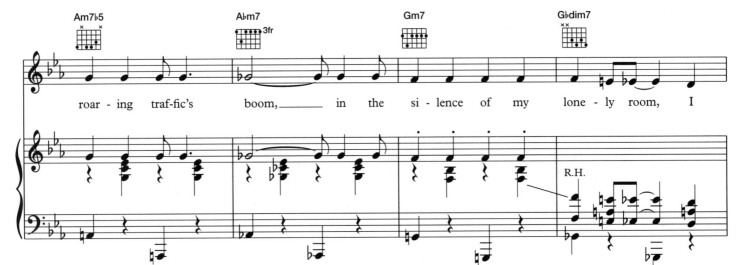

oh, such a hun-gry yearn - ing burn-ing in - side of me,＿＿＿＿ and it's

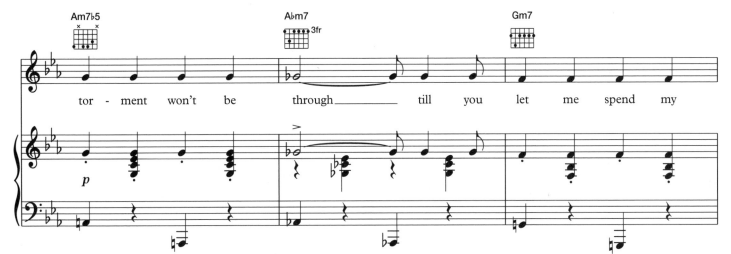

tor - ment won't be through＿＿＿ till you let me spend my

life mak-ing love＿ to you, day and night,＿＿＿＿ night and day.＿

Night and day ＿＿＿＿＿＿＿＿＿＿

8vb

LULLABY OF BROADWAY

Words by AL DUBIN
Music by HARRY WARREN

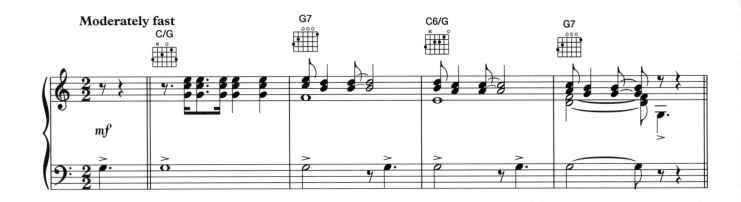

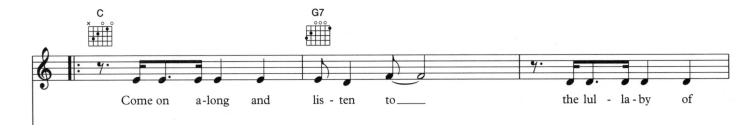

Come on a-long and lis-ten to___ the lul-la-by of

Broad-way,

the hip hoo-ray and bal-ly-hoo,___
the hi-dee-hi and boop-a-doo,___

MARTA

Words by L WOLFE GILBERT
Music by MOISES SIMONS

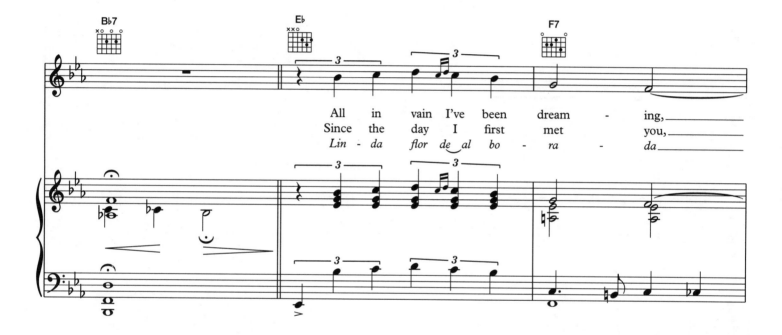

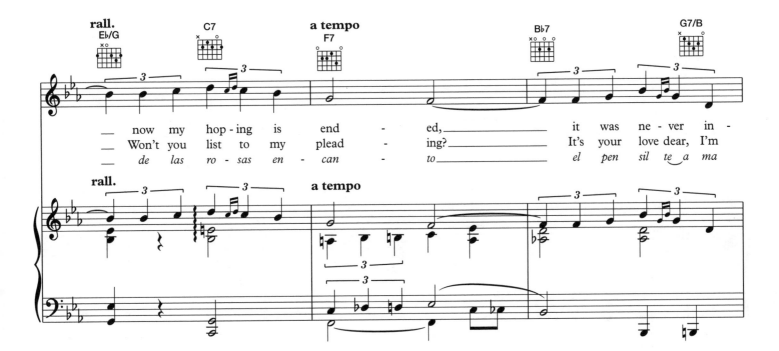

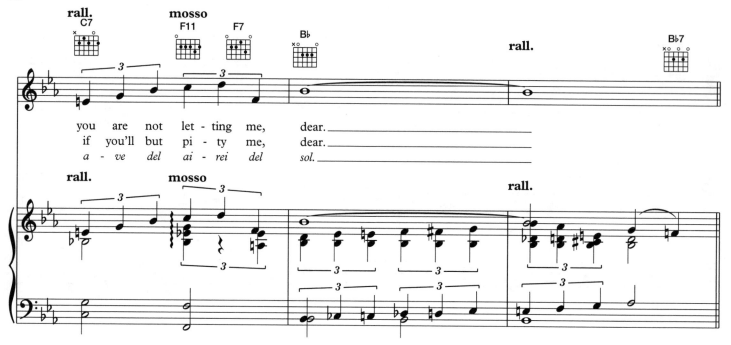

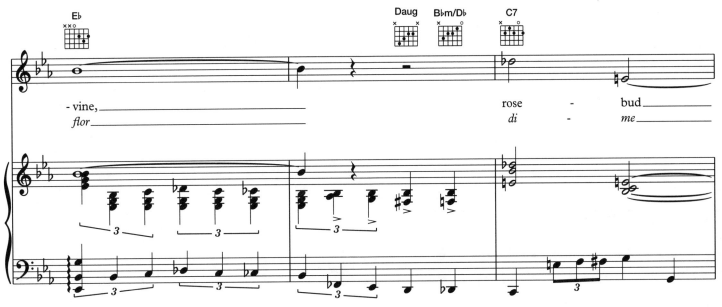

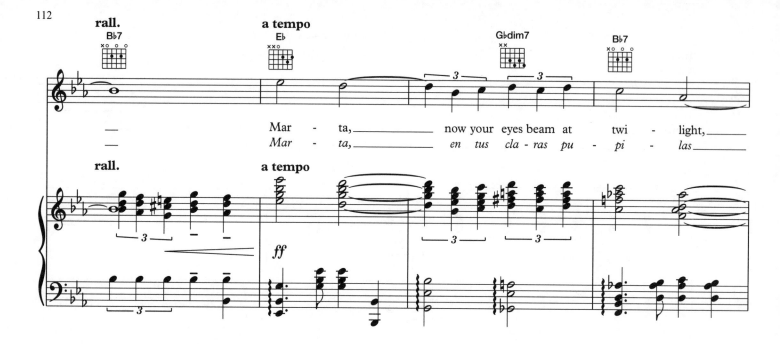

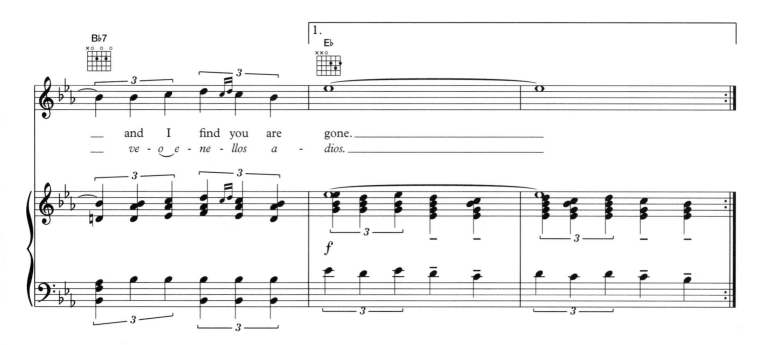

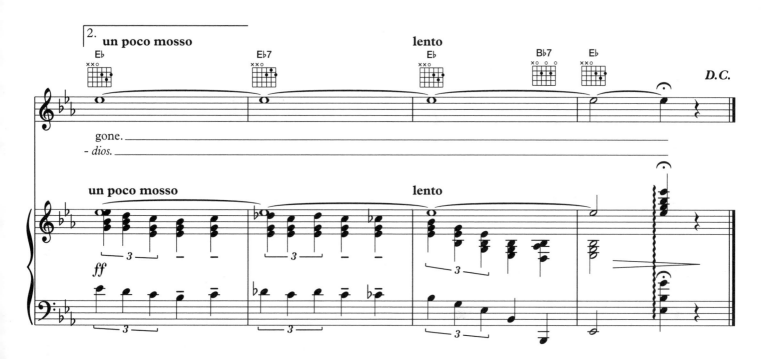

MY FUNNY VALENTINE

Words by LORENZ HART
Music by RICHARD RODGERS

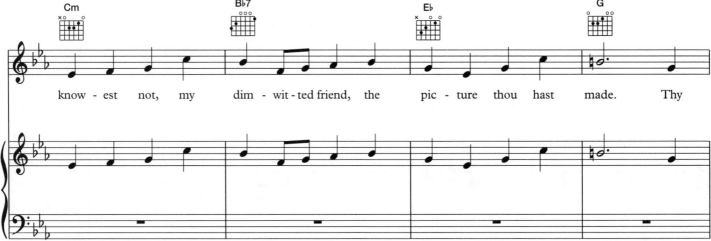

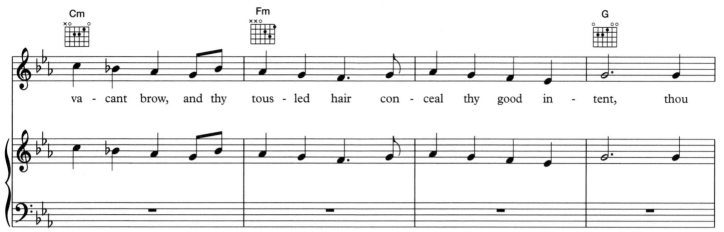

va - cant brow, and thy tous - led hair con - ceal thy good in - tent, thou

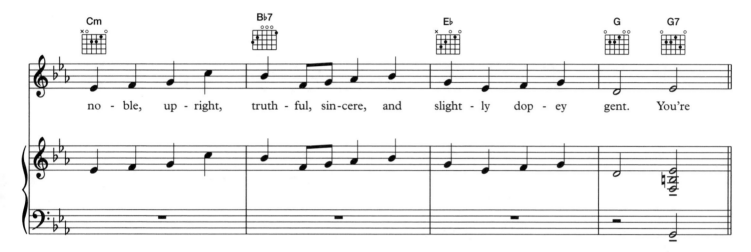

no - ble, up - right, truth - ful, sin - cere, and slight - ly dop - ey gent. You're

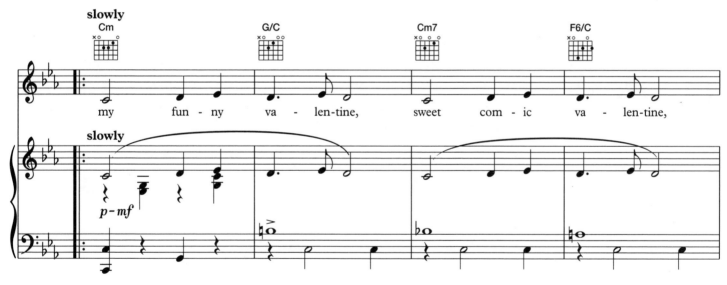

slowly

my fun - ny va - len - tine, sweet com - ic va - len - tine,

slowly

p - mf

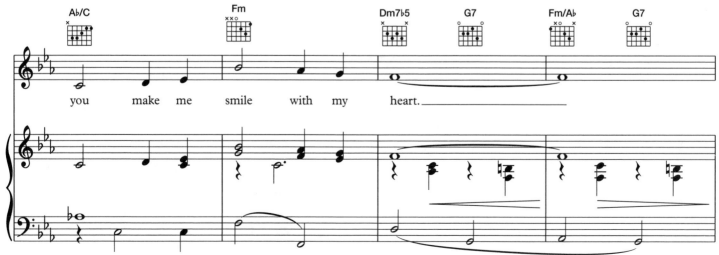

you make me smile with my heart.

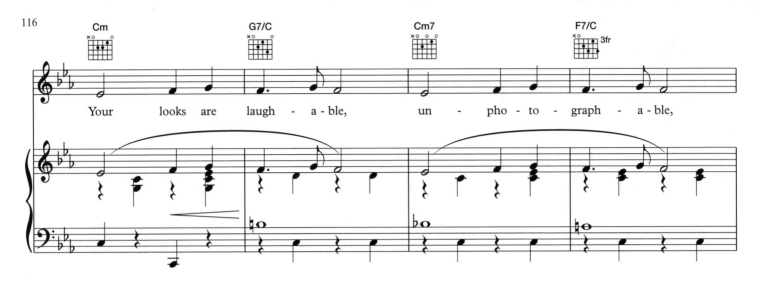

Your looks are laugh - a - ble, un - pho - to - graph - a - ble,

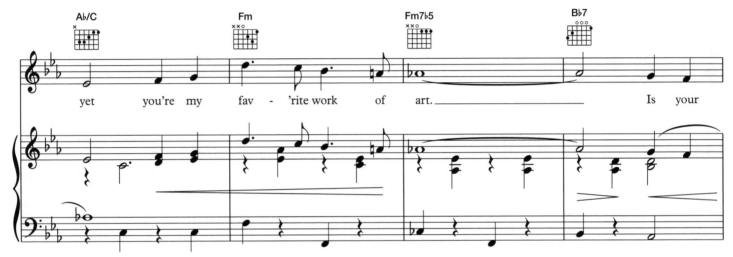

yet you're my fav - 'rite work of art._____ Is your

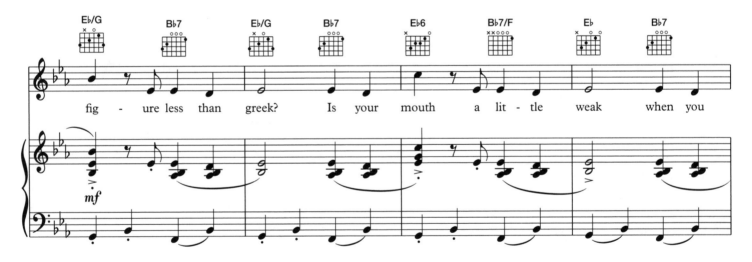

fig - ure less than greek? Is your mouth a lit - tle weak when you

o - pen it to speak? Are you smart?_____ But

MY PRAYER

Words by JIMMY KENEDY
Music by GEORGE BOULANGER

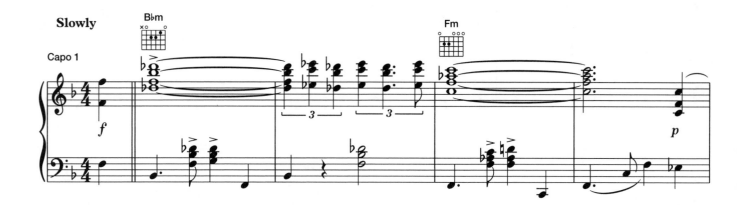

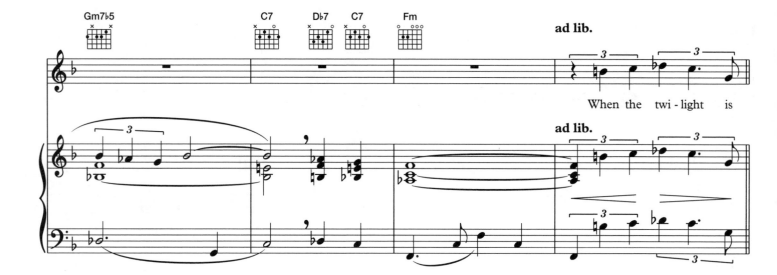

When the twi - light is

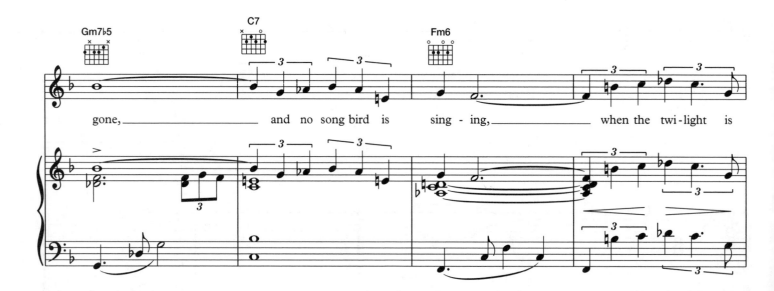

gone, _____ and no song bird is sing - ing, _____ when the twi - light is

OLD FATHER THAMES

Words by RAY WALLACE
Music by BETSY O'HOGAN

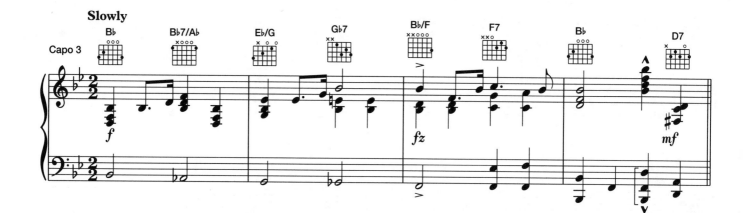

There's some folks___ who al - ways wor - ry, and
The best way,___ a hea - ven-blessed way, just

some folks___ who ne - ver care, but in this world of rush and hur - ry, it
try to___ be al - ways kind. It does - n't mat - ter what the rest say, you're

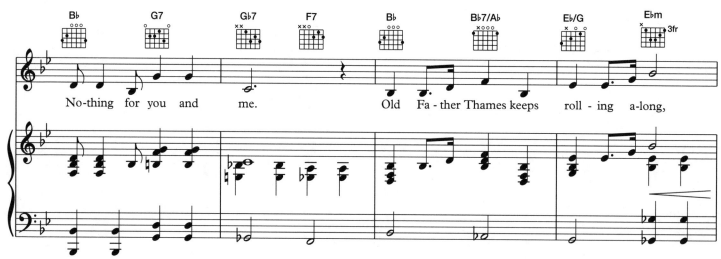

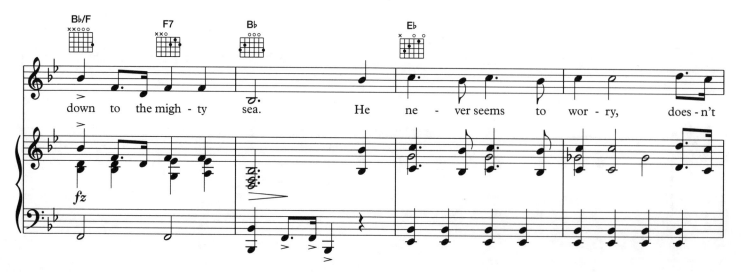

SALLY

Words and Music by WILL HAINES,
HARRY LEON and LEO TOWERS

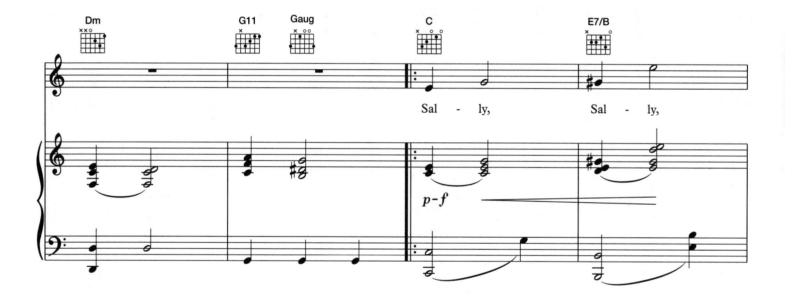

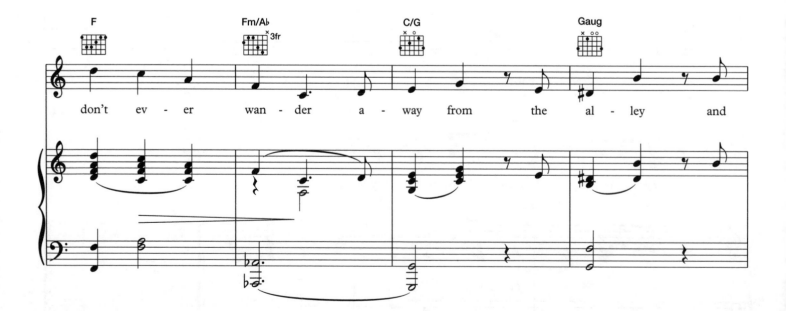

SING AS WE GO

Words and Music by HARRY PARR-DAVIES

Bright march tempo

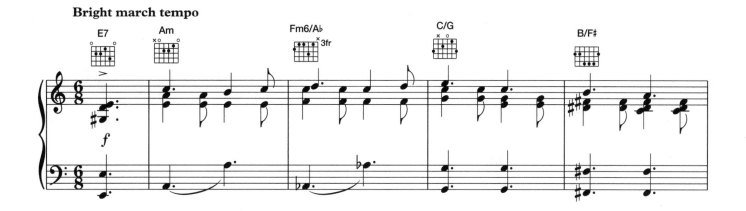

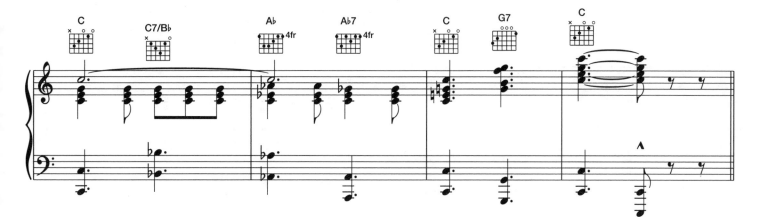

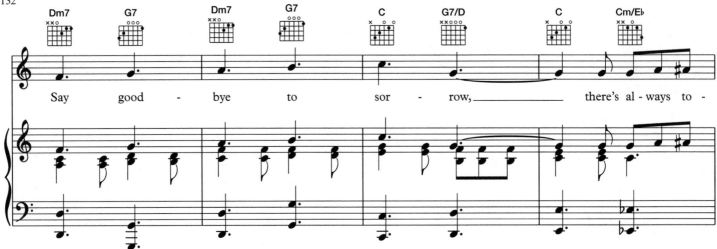

Say good - bye to sor - row,_____ there's al - ways to -

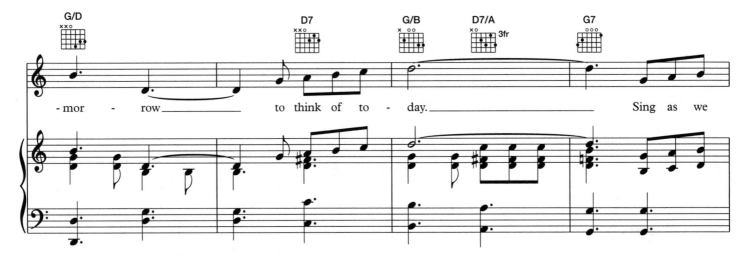

- mor - row_____ to think of to - day._____ Sing as we

go_____ al - though the skies are grey,_____

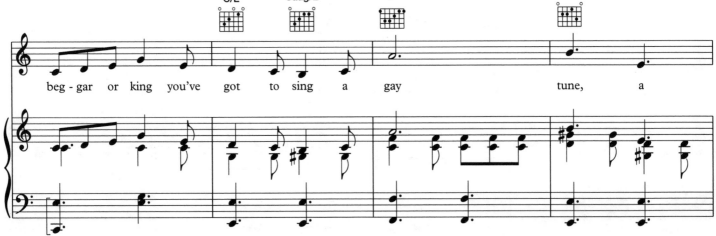

beg - gar or king you've got to sing a gay tune, a

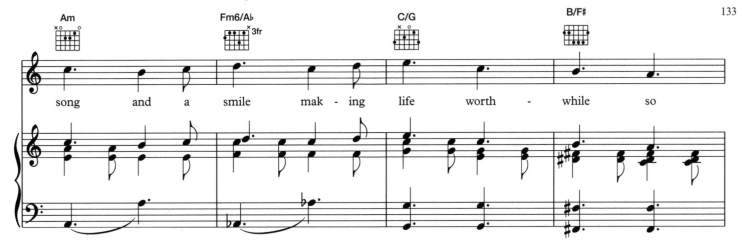

song and a smile mak-ing life worth-while so

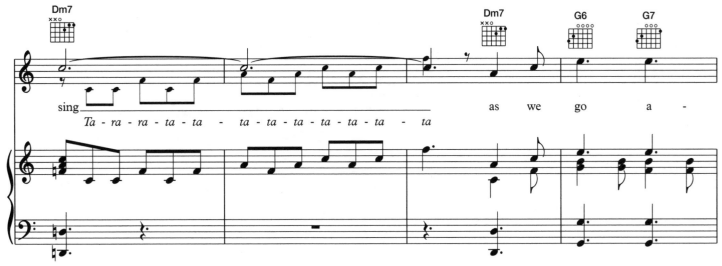

sing _Ta-ra-ra-ta-ta - ta-ta-ta-ta-ta-ta - ta_ as we go a-

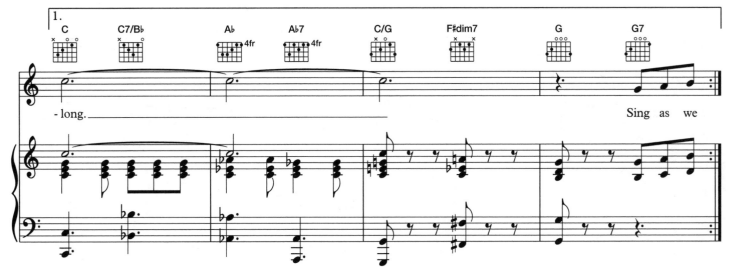

1.

-long. Sing as we

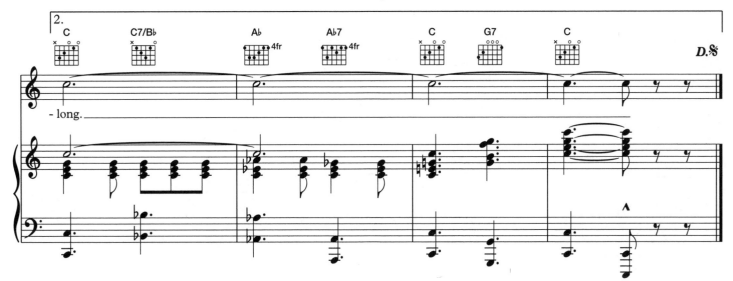

2.

-long.

STORMY WEATHER

Words by TED KOEHLER
Music by HAROLD ARLEN

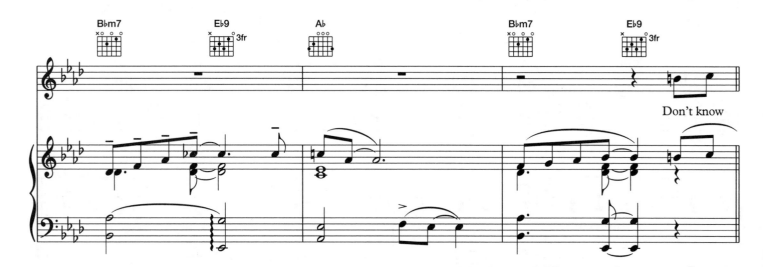

Don't know

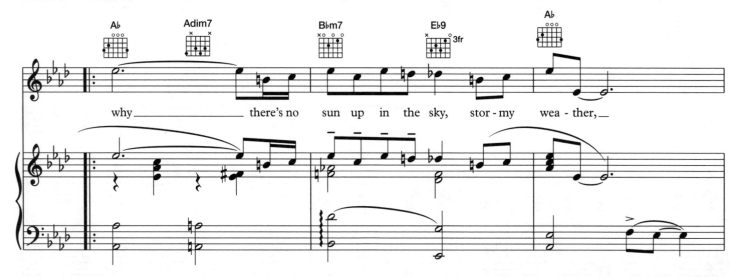

why _____ there's no sun up in the sky, stor-my wea-ther,_

since my man and I_____ ain't to - ge - ther,_____ keeps rain - in' all___ the

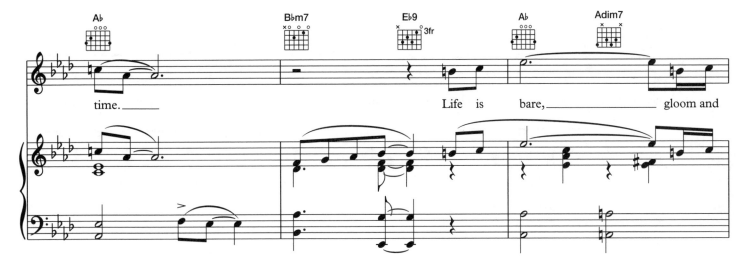

time._____ Life is bare,_____ gloom and

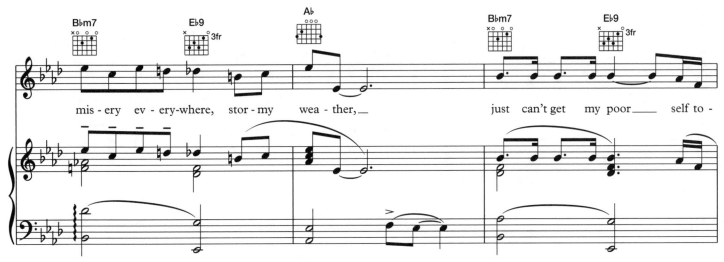

mis - ery ev - ery-where, stor - my wea - ther,_ just can't get my poor___ self to -

- ge - ther,_____ I'm wea - ry all___ the time,_____ the

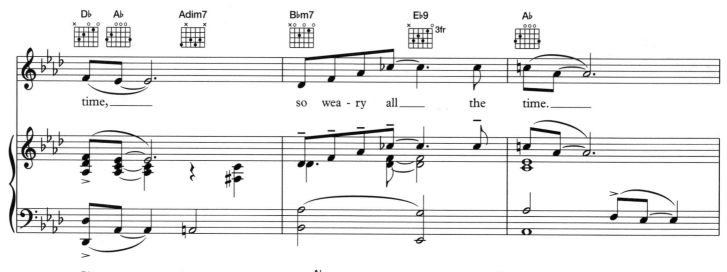

time,_____ so wea-ry all___ the time._____

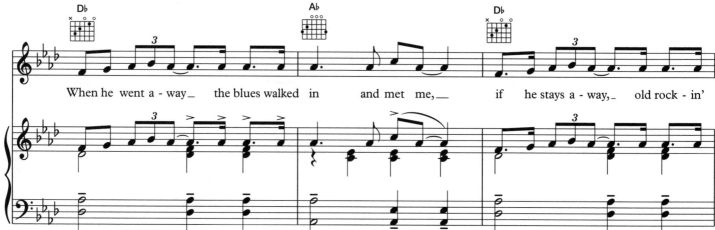

When he went a-way___ the blues walked in and met me,___ if he stays a-way,___ old rock-in'

chair will get me.___ All I do is pray___ the Lord a-bove will let me___

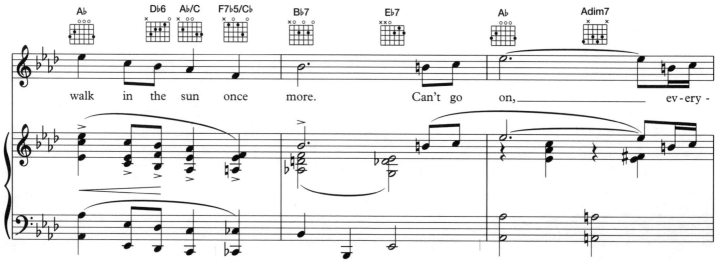

walk in the sun once more. Can't go on,_____ ev-ery-

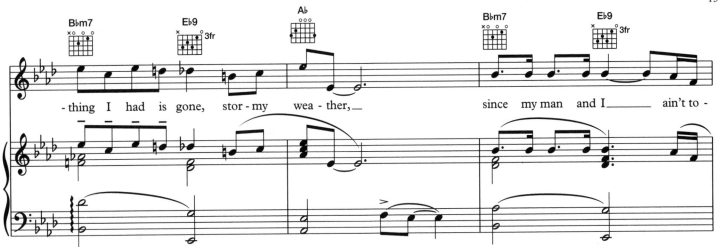

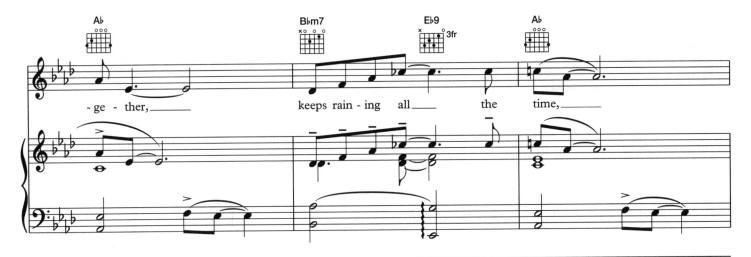

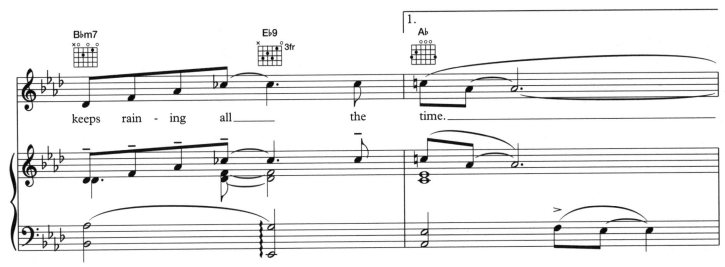

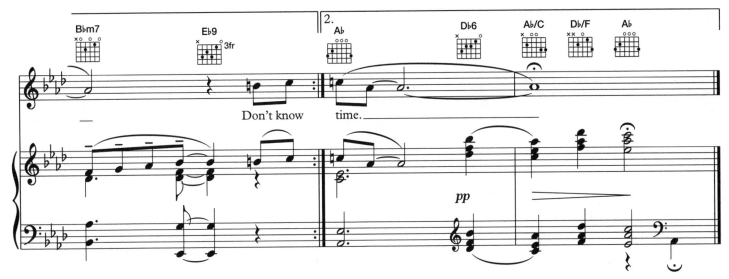

SUMMERTIME

Music and Lyrics by GEORGE GERSHWIN,
DUBOSE and DOROTHY HEYWARD and IRA GERSHWIN

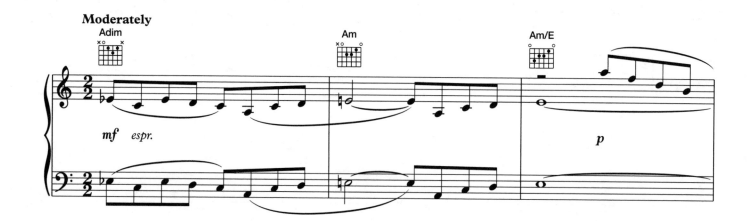

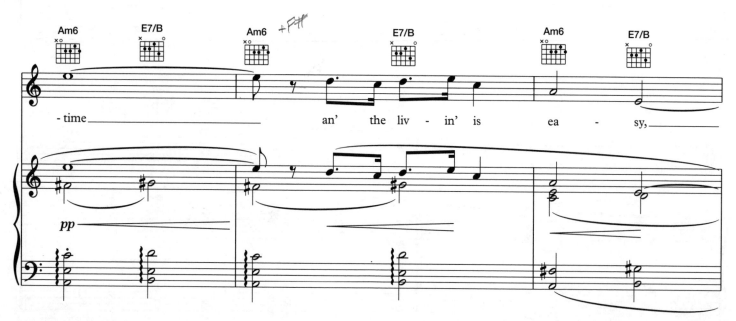

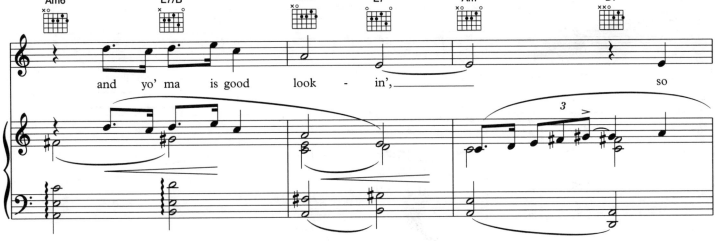

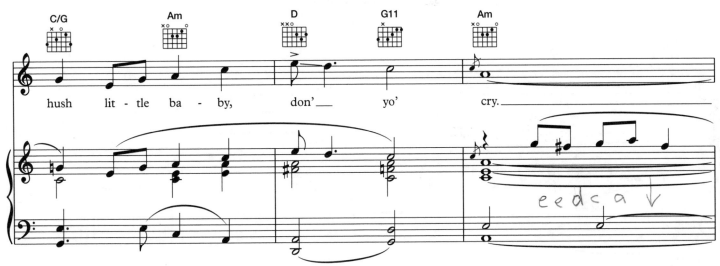

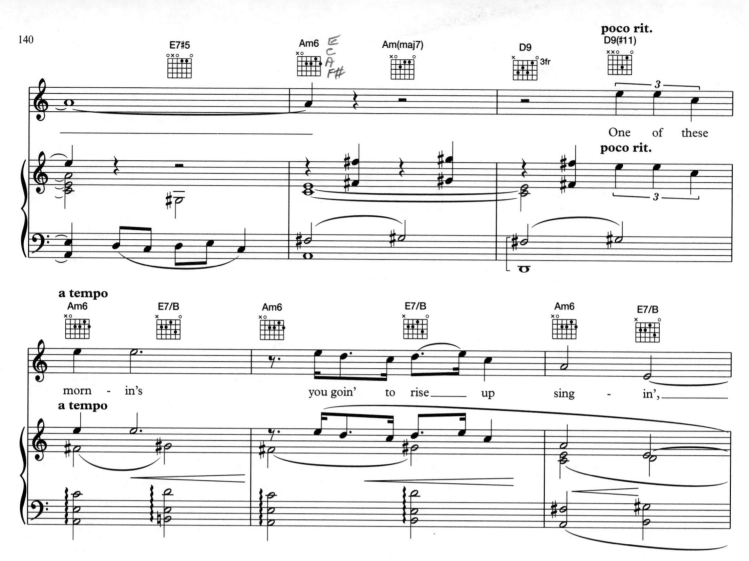

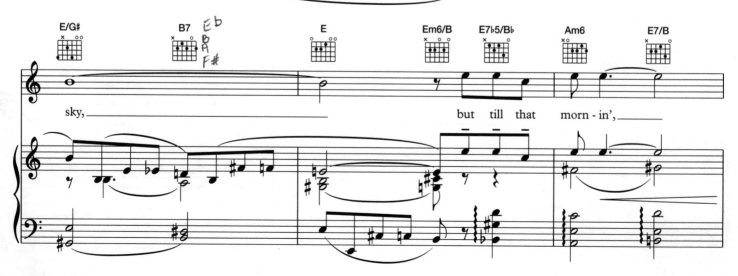

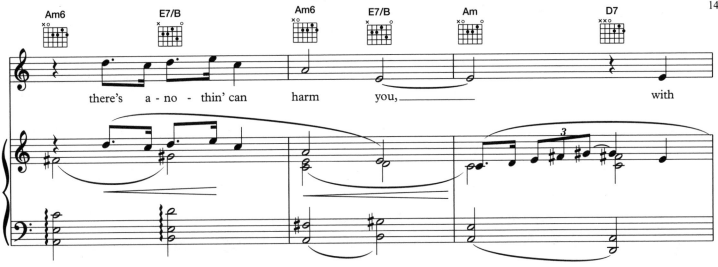

there's a - no - thin' can harm you,_____ with

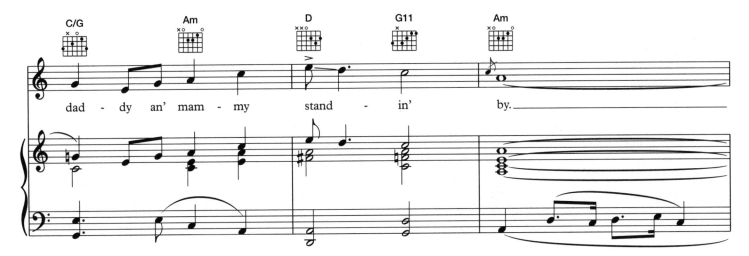

dad - dy an' mam - my stand - in' by._____

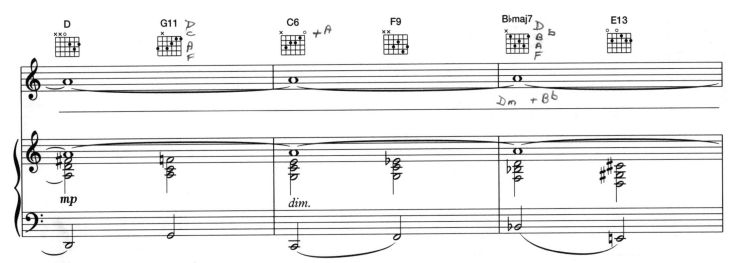

SWEET AND LOVELY

Words and Music by GUS ARNHEIM,
HARRY TOBIAS and JULES LEMARE

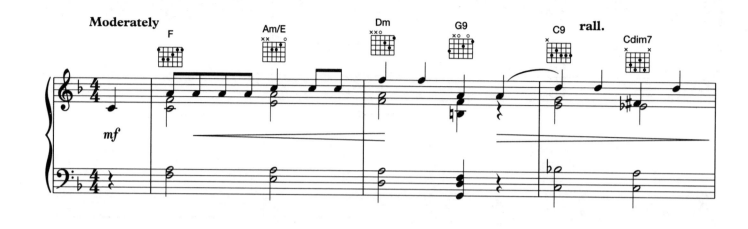

THEY CAN'T TAKE THAT AWAY FROM ME

Music and Lyrics by GEORGE GERSHWIN and IRA GERSHWIN

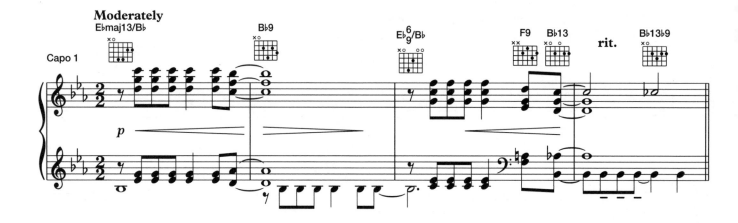

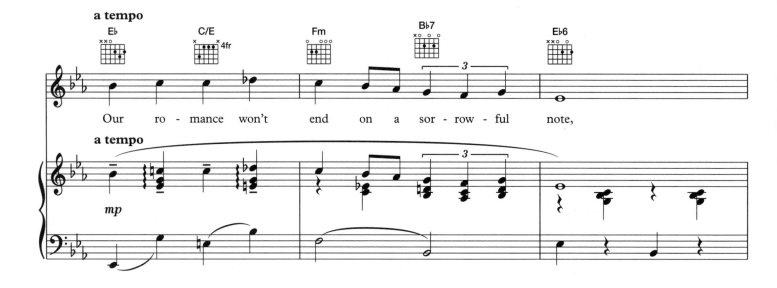

Our ro-mance won't end on a sor-row-ful note,

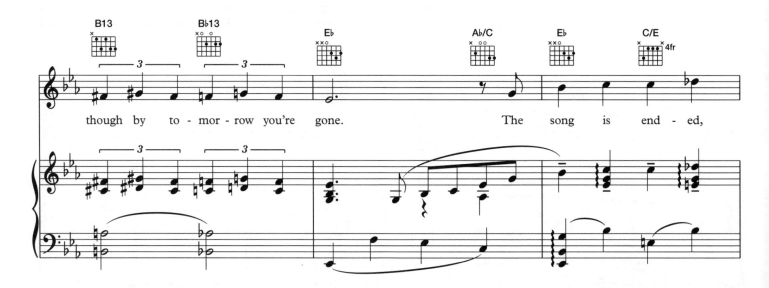

though by to-mor-row you're gone. The song is end-ed,

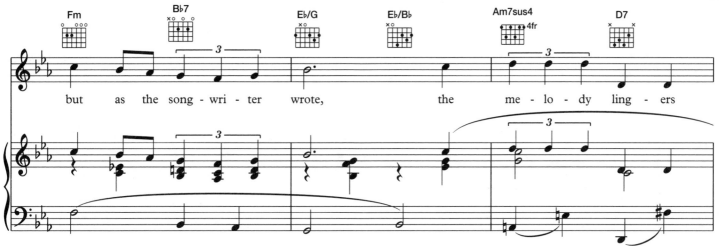

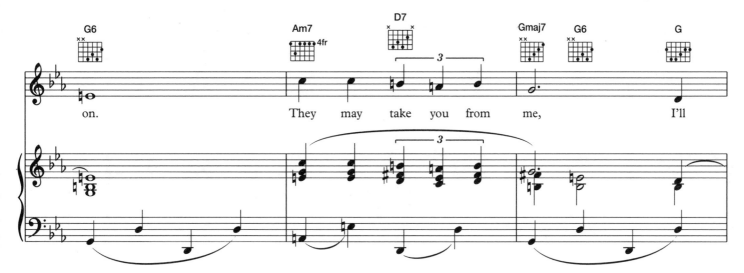

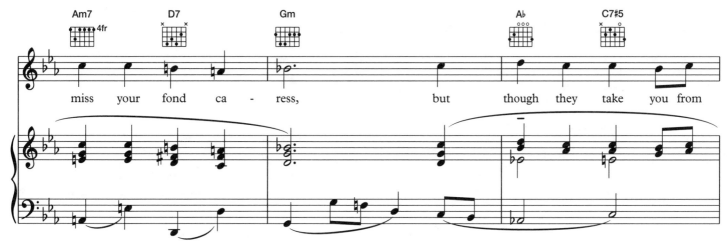

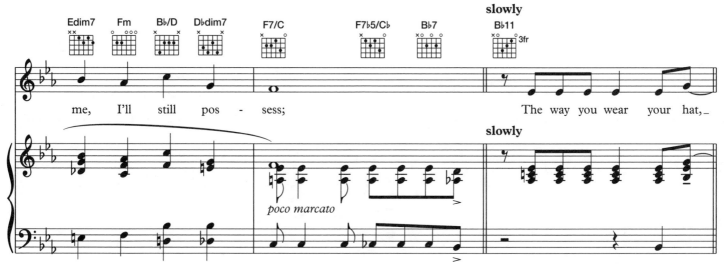

WALTZING IN THE CLOUDS

Original Words by ERNST MARISCHKA
English Words by GUS KAHN
Music by ROBERT STOLZ

Lyrics:

I was a mor-tal with feet on the ground,
there I was stand-ing with peo-ple a-round.

What if I fell for the spell of a dance,
lead-ing me in-to a world of ro-mance?

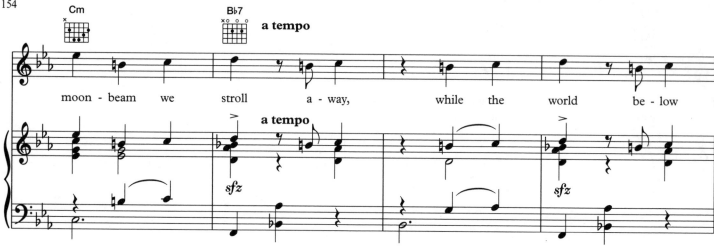

moon - beam we stroll a - way, while the world be - low

seems to roll a - way, and we go waltz - ing,

waltz - ing high in the clouds, on - ly you and

I in the clouds, no one will hear when you

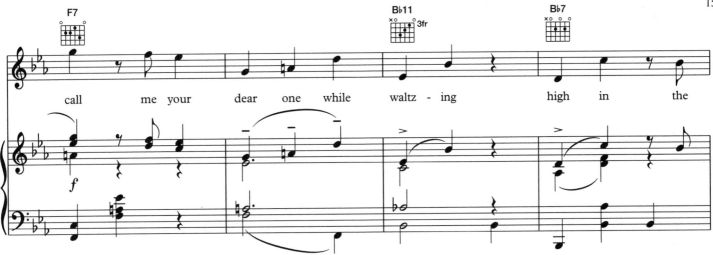

call me your dear one while waltz - ing high in the

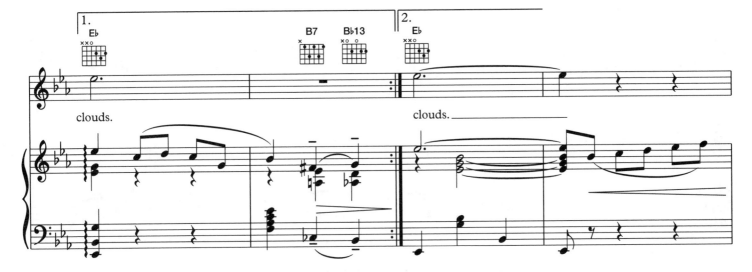

clouds. clouds.

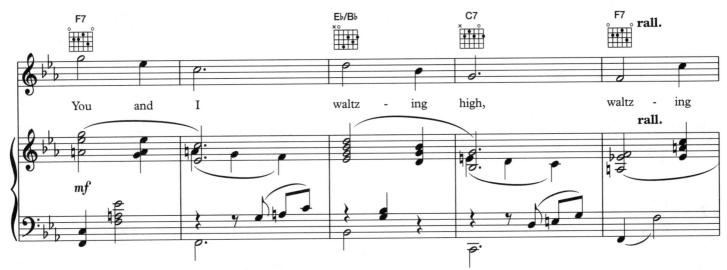

You and I waltz - ing high, waltz - ing

in the clouds.

TWO SLEEPY PEOPLE

Words by FRANK LOESSER
Music by HOAGY CARMICHAEL

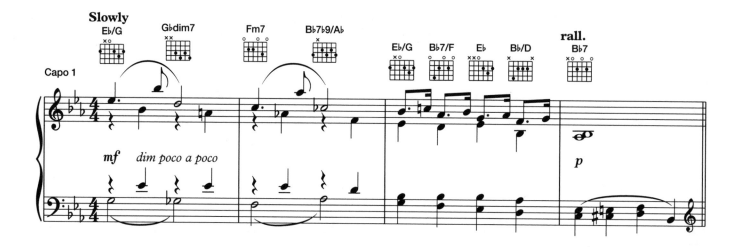

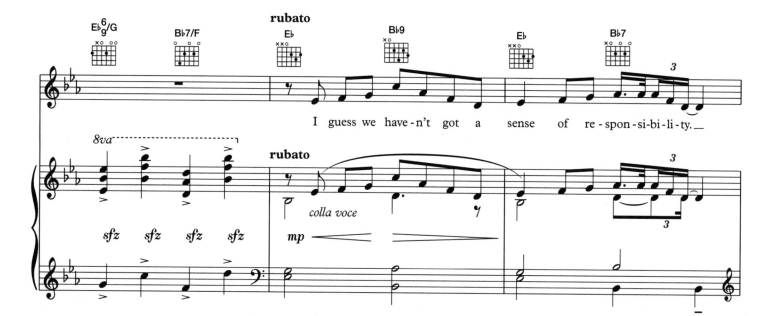

I guess we have-n't got a sense of re-spon-si-bi-li-ty.

Our young ro-mance is so in-tense, we're close to

in the co-zy chair,_ pick-ing on a wish-bone from the Fri-gid-aire,_

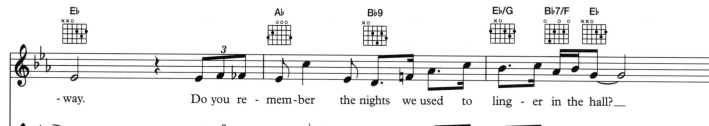

two slee-py peo-ple with no-thing to say, and too much in love to break a-

-way. Do you re-mem-ber the nights we used to ling-er in the hall?_

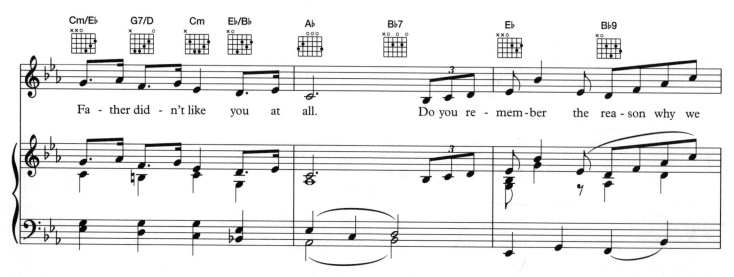

Fa-ther did-n't like you at all. Do you re-mem-ber the rea-son why we

WHEN SOMEBODY THINKS YOU'RE WONDERFUL

Words and Music by HARRY WOODS

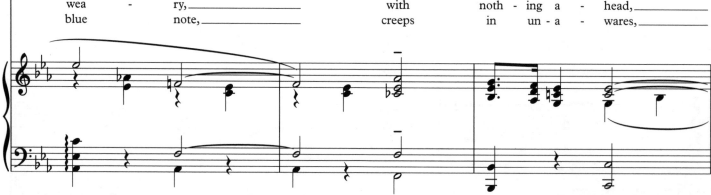

Time goes a - long,___ you're a - lone and
Life is a song,___ but some-times a

wea - ry,___ with noth - ing a - head,___
blue note,___ creeps in un - a - wares,___

poco rit.

a tempo

you.
- ly.

Is - n't it true?__
Don't you a - gree?__

When some-bo-dy thinks you're

won - der-ful,

what a diff-erence in__ your day.

Seems as though your trou - bles dis - ap-pear,

like a fea-ther in__ your

way. When some-bo-dy thinks you're won - der-ful,

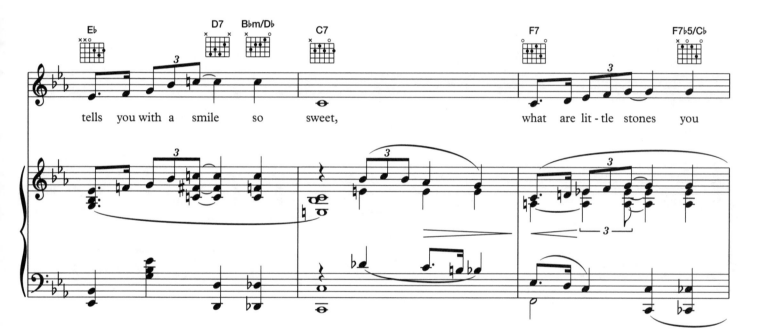

tells you with a smile so sweet, what are lit-tle stones you

step up-on, just a mea-dow 'neath your feet, and

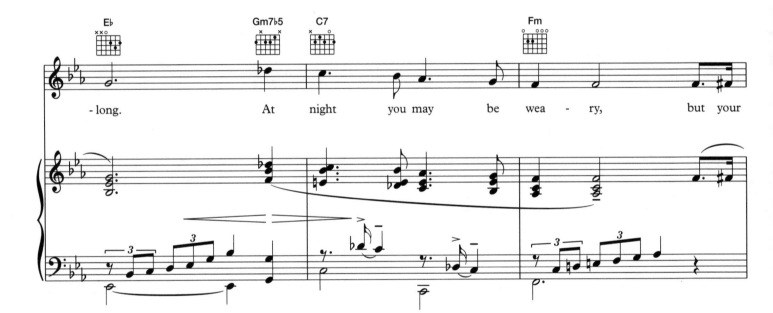

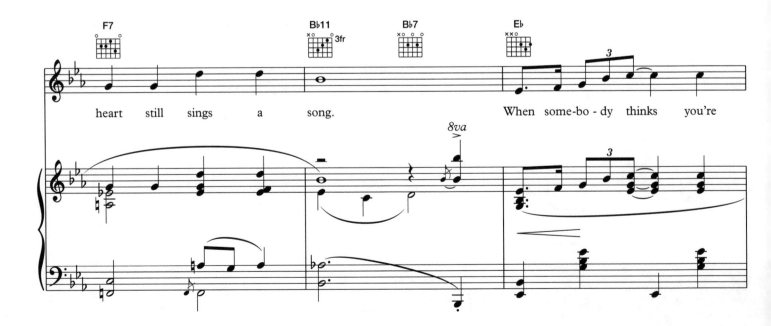

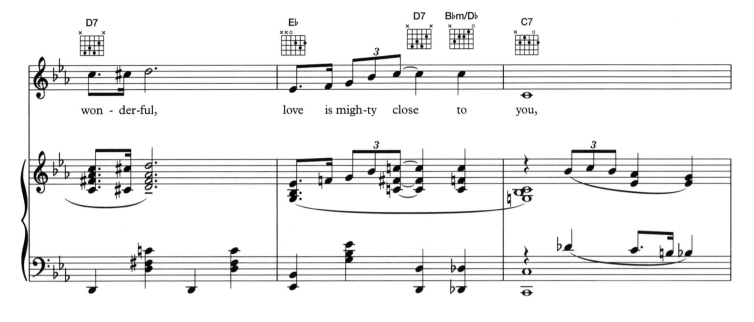

won - der-ful,   love is migh-ty close to   you,

just an - oth - er thing___ more won - der - ful,

mak - ing all her dreams come true.   true.

D.C.

WINTER WONDERLAND

Words by RICHARD B SMITH
Music by FELIX BERNARD

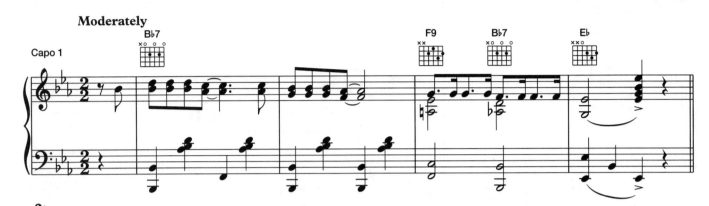

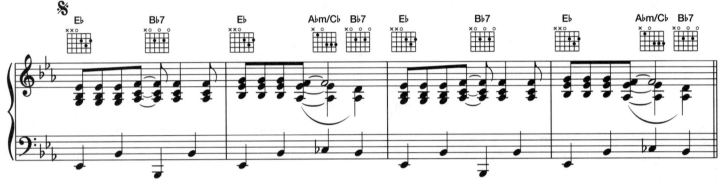

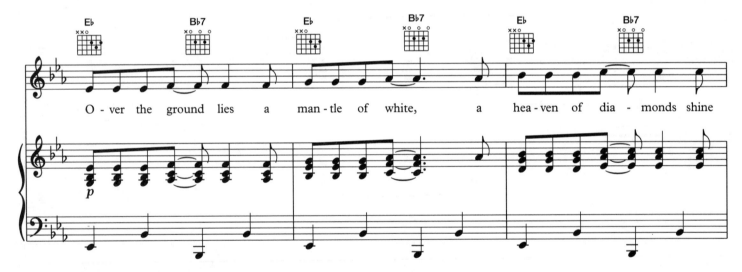

Over the ground lies a man-tle of white, a hea-ven of dia-monds shine

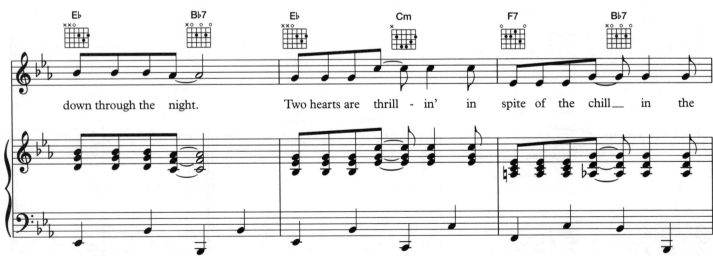

down through the night. Two hearts are thrill-in' in spite of the chill__ in the

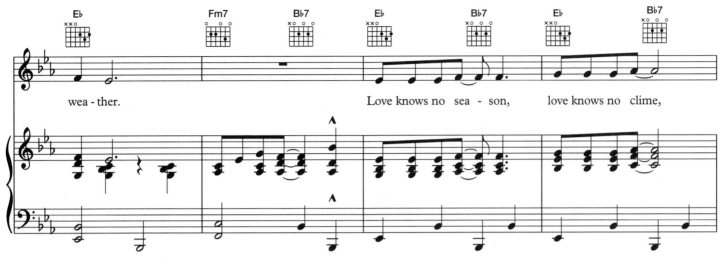

wea - ther. Love knows no sea - son, love knows no clime,

ro-mance can blos - som a - ny old time,__ here in the o - pen, we're

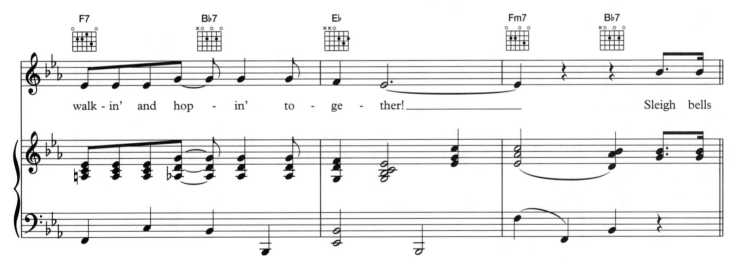

walk - in' and hop - in' to - ge - ther!_____ Sleigh bells

ring, are you lis - t'nin'? In the lane, snow is glist - 'nin', a

Brown.____ He'll say, 'Are you mar-ried?' We'll say, 'No, man! But

you can do the job when you're in town!' La-ter on, we'll con-spire__ as we

dream by the fire,__ to face un-a-fraid_ the plans that we made

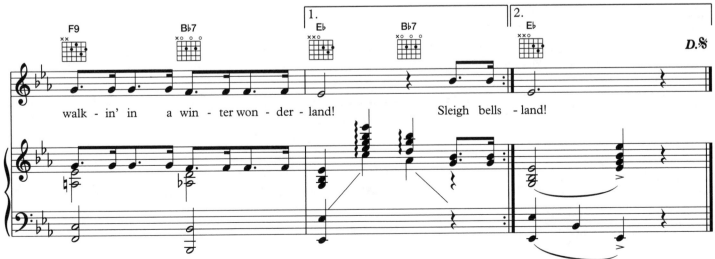

walk-in' in a win-ter won-der-land! Sleigh bells -land!

YOU GO TO MY HEAD

Words by HAVEN GILLESPIE
Music by J FRED COOTS

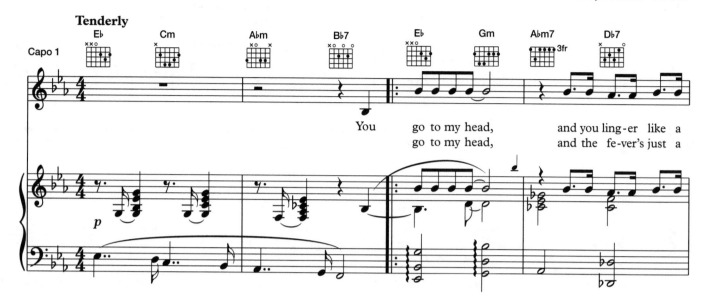

171

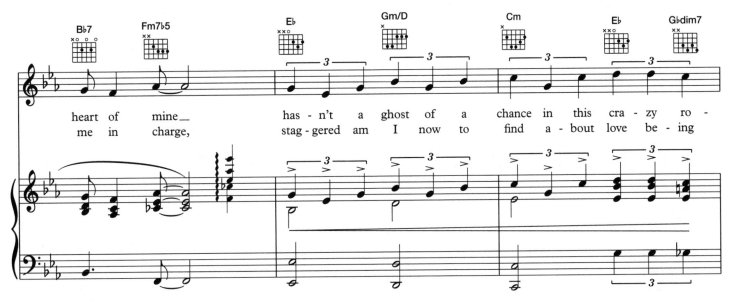

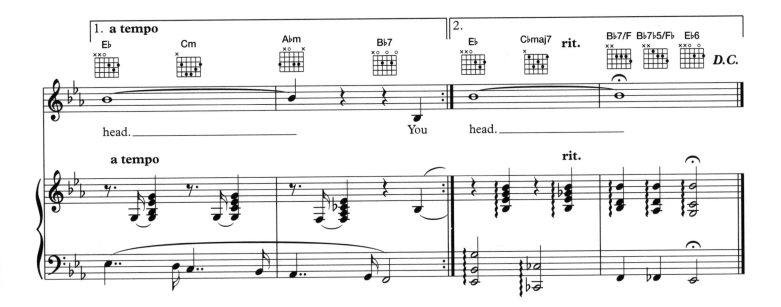

WHEN YOUR OLD WEDDING RING WAS NEW

Words by CHARLES McCARTHY and JOE SOLIERI
Music by BERT DOUGLAS

old wed-ding ring was new,_____ and each

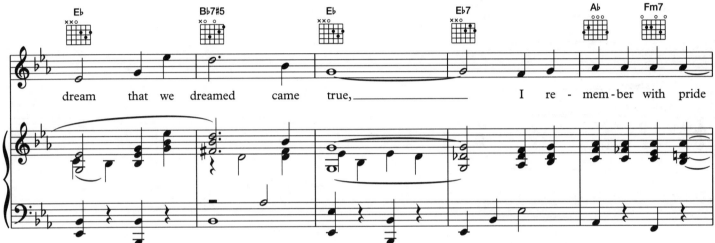

dream that we dreamed came true,_____ I re-mem-ber with pride

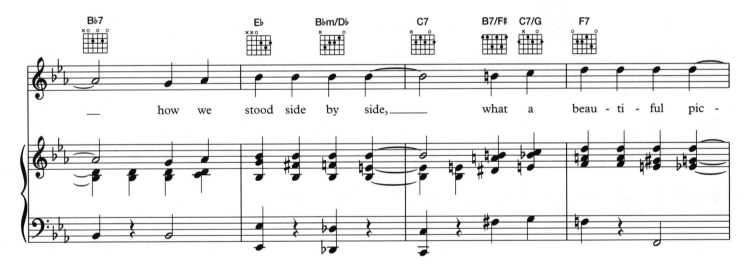

___ how we stood side by side,_____ what a beau-ti-ful pic-

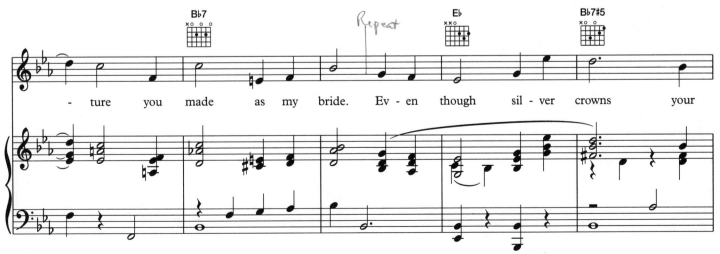

-ture you made as my bride. Ev-en though sil-ver crowns your